Praise for Guitar for Beginners

Great beginner book

"This is a great book. When you're starting off you don't know, what you don't know... And this covers everything. So read it cover to cover first. There's so many gaps this filled in. Also there are audio files and youtube video links that go along with the songs and licks... That way you can see it in the book and hear it... Makes it so much easier to reproduce it. The only downside is you may outgrow this book fairly quickly... But that's a good thing, so you can move on to more advanced books"

— *Utax*

Just what I was looking for!

"I know there are so many videos online and it's best to have a teacher, but I love to learn from books and this was the perfect supplement to my super-beginner guitar education! And it's true- I WAS able to play a song in 7 days!! (Spoiler: it's "Happy Birthday") I feel like this book has given me a solid foundation of the basics and it made the guitar not scary and mysterious! Thank you, Guitar Head!"

— *M. Daley*

Guitar head you dunnit again

"This book has really made a difference to my learning how to play that that thing, 20 years ago I picked up a guitar and put it down again weeks later, three months ago i picked up the same guitar and it has been my daily companion and so many tanks to Guitar Head for his understanding of our weaknesses when it comes to learning , this is a book that I would highly recommend to those of you who want to learn to play,,,,,, give it a go, disappointment wont come into the equation cheers"

— *Bill*

Guitar for Beginners

How to Play Your First Song In 7 Days Even If You've Never Picked Up A Guitar

GH@theguitarhead.com

www.facebook.com/theguitarhead/

©Copyright 2021 by Guitar Head — All rights reserved.

This document is geared towards providing exact and reliable information in regard to the topic and issue covered. The publication is sold with the idea that the publisher is not required to render accounting, officially permitted, or otherwise, qualified services. If advice is necessary, legal or professional, a practiced individual in the profession should be ordered.

From a Declaration of Principles which was accepted and approved equally by a Committee of the American Bar Association and a Committee of Publishers and Associations.

In no way is it legal to reproduce, duplicate, or transmit any part of this document in either electronic means or in printed format. Recording of this publication is strictly prohibited and any storage of this document is not allowed unless with written permission from the publisher. All rights reserved.

The information provided herein is stated to be truthful and consistent, in that any liability, in terms of inattention or otherwise, by any usage or abuse of any policies, processes, or directions contained within is the solitary and utter responsibility of the recipient reader. Under no circumstances will any legal responsibility or blame be held against the publisher for any reparation, damages, or monetary loss due to the information herein, either directly or indirectly.

Respective authors own all copyrights not held by the publisher.

The information herein is offered for informational purposes solely and is universal as so. The presentation of the information is without a contract or any type of guarantee assurance.

The trademarks that are used are without any consent, and the publication of the trademark is without permission or backing by the trademark owner. All trademarks and brands within this book are for clarifying purposes only and are owned by the owners themselves, not affiliated with this document.

Disclaimer

Please note the information contained within this document is for educational and entertainment purposes only. Every attempt has been made to provide accurate, up to date and reliable complete information. No warranties of any kind are expressed or implied. Readers acknowledge that the author is not engaging in the rendering of legal and financial, medical or professional advice. The content of this book has been derived from various sources. Please consult a licensed professional before attempting any techniques outlined in this book.

By reading this document, the reader agrees that under no circumstances are is the author responsible for any losses, direct or indirect, which are incurred as a result of the use of the information contained within this document, including, but not limited to, — errors, omissions, or inaccuracies.

Dedication

*We dedicate this book to the complete
Guitar Head team,
supporters, well-wishers and
the Guitar Head community.*

*It goes without saying that we
would not have gotten
this far without
your encouragement,
critique and support.*

Contents

Free Guitar Head Bonuses 8

Part 1 : The First 7 Days of Your Journey 11

Introduction 12

Day 1 : The Basic Stuff... plus Tuning and Your First Melody 15
    Parts of the Guitar 15
    How to Hold the Guitar 17
    How to Hold a Pick 21
    How to Tune Your Guitar 23
    Your First Melody 27
    Guitar Tablature — What It Is and How to Use It 31

Day 2 : More Melodies... 38
    How much should I practice? 40
    Finger Exercises 42
    Sore fingers? 44
    Bonus Melodies 45

Day 3 : Your First Chords 48

Days 4 & 5 : Mastering Chord Shifting 54
    Mastering the Shift 54
    The 2 Chord Shift 57

Day 6 : Playing with the Right Rhythm 59
    Set the Beat 59
    Other Time Signatures 60
    Strumming 61
    Understanding the metronome 66
    Take a rest.... 67

Day 7 : Your First Song 68
    Time for some real songs!! 68
    Bonus Songs 72
    Other Popular Songs You Can Play 75

Part 2 : Taking Your Playing to the Next Level.... 79

What do I get to learn in the 2nd part?. 80

Chapter 1 : Other Open Chords...(Yes, There's More!!). 82
    Major Chords. 82
    Minor Chords. 83
    Dominant Seventh Chords 85
    Bonus Songs 88
    Other popular songs to play using all these new chords. 90

Chapter 2 : Rhythm and Strumming. 92
    How to Begin to Understand Rhythm in Music. 93
    The Different Types of Notes and Their Rhythms 93
    The Different Types of Rests and Their Rhythms 96
    What Exactly is a Time Signature?. 98
    Some Examples of Counting and Strumming 100

CHAPTER 3 : F chord and B chord 106
    Some Basic Chord Shapes. 107
    Let's improve the chord with an exercise 109
    Move them around... 110
    Here are some more... 110

CHAPTER 4 : What is a Scale?. 112
    The Musical Alphabet 112
    But Aren't There More Notes Than That?. 113
    Sharps and Flats. 113
    From 12 Back to 7. 116
    Keys Unlock it All 119
    How Keys and Scales Work Together 120

CHAPTER 5 : What are Intervals?. 122
    A Quick Note on Playing Intervals. 122
    Intervals of a Second 123
    Intervals of a Third 123
    The Perfect Fourth. 124
    Intervals of a Fifth. 125
    Intervals of a Sixth 126
    Intervals of a Seventh 127
    The Octave 128

CHAPTER 6 : Some Useful Exercises. 129
    Alternate Picking. 130

What Next?. 134

Farewell!. 135

Free Guitar Head Bonuses

Audio Files

All Guitar Head books come with audio tracks for the licks inside the book. These audio tracks are an integral part of the book - they ensure you are playing the charts and chords the way they are intended to be played.

Lifetime access to Guitar Head Community

Being around like-minded people is the first step to being successful at anything. The Guitar Head community is a place where you can find people who are willing to listen to your music, answer your questions or talk anything guitar.

Email newsletters sent directly to your inbox

We send regular guitar lessons and tips to all our subscribers. Our subscribers are also the first to know about Guitar Head giveaways and holiday discounts.

Free PDF

Guitar mastery is all about the details! Getting the small things right and avoiding mistakes that can slow your guitar journey by years. So, we wrote a book about 25 of the most common mistakes guitarists make and decided to give it for free to all Guitar Head readers.

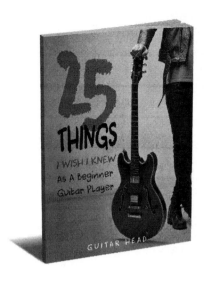

You can grab a copy of the free book, audio files and subscribe to newsletter by following the link below.

All these bonuses are a 100% free, with no strings attached. You won't need to enter any personal details other than your first name and email address.

To get your bonuses, go to: ***www.theguitarhead.com/bonus***

PART 1

The First 7 Days of Your Journey

Introduction

There is no shortage of claims out in the world — either in printed books or on the internet — that says you can learn how to play the guitar almost overnight. They make it sound like all you have to do is learn a few tricks in just a few minutes and you'll be on your way to being a seasoned pro.

Well, I'm here to tell you... *they're right.*

Yep. You heard me right. They are absolutely correct.

In fact, if you take the time to read this book, I can have you playing the guitar (I mean really playing the guitar) within just seven short days. And I'm going to do it without all of the boring music theory that will get you to sleep faster than a big turkey dinner topped off with a glass of warm milk.

How will I do that, you ask?

Let me explain...

Yes, learning the guitar can be boring. Yes, learning the guitar can be tedious. But if you can form a method that takes those boring topics out to present things in a streamlined process — everyone can actually be playing songs in a few days.

If you carefully follow the directions I have laid out over a seven-day period, when the 7th day wraps up you'll be able to:

- ✓ Play simple open chords
- ✓ Learn to play them together to actually play a song
- ✓ Be able to identify all of the parts of a guitar

- Know how to read chord charts and guitar tablature (tab is God's gift to guitarists, by the way...)

I know what you're thinking: "This sounds great! Let's get going!"

But........................

There's the catch.

You just *knew* there was going to be a catch, right?

"Playing guitar" is a pretty broad statement. You will be able to say that you are "playing guitar" just by learning the beginner topics that we are going to go over. The catch is that you have to approach playing the guitar with reasonable expectations.

Let's face it, you aren't going to be able to play Van Halen's "Eruption", Led Zeppelin's "Stairway to Heaven", or the Eagles' "Hotel California" in a week. Sorry — it's just not happening like that. Not unless you are some sort of alien freak that can play like Steve Vai or John McLaughlin right out of the box...

But here's the deal:

- You *will* know how to play some single note melodies.
- You *will* be able to know some chords.
- You *will* be able to play a few songs.
- You *will* know more about guitar than 99% of your friends, and you will be able to impress the heck out of them at your next party.

How does that sound? It would sound pretty good to me...I wish someone would have guided and encouraged me like this when I started playing at eleven years old.

And... that's just Part 1 of the book!

In Part 2 I'll go into a much deeper dive on some of the topics that you'll need to know to take your playing past the basics and develop into the intermediate phase — and beyond.

Topics that we will go over include:

- More advanced chord shapes such as barre chords.
- Learning your first scale!
- Some advanced theory topics.
- Some useful exercises.

In Part 2 I don't have a particular timeframe for learning each chapter and/or topic as we have in Part 1. Part 1 is the jump start, and Part 2 is the slow, steady acceleration that will get your playing up to 100 MPH on the freeway. How fast is that acceleration? Whatever you feel most comfortable with where you will really grasp the material and make it your own.

So? What do you think? Are you ready?

I am…

So, strap yourself in, my friend, because here…we……*go!!*

DAY 1

The Basic Stuff... plus Tuning and Your First Melody

(...you gotta start somewhere, right?...)

So here we are... Day 1...

Nervous?

Nah. Don't be. I'm here to help guide you through this.

I will give you a heads-up though: you'll find that some of the days have more reading while some have quite a bit less, but more things to actually practice. I'd recommend not skipping to the good stuff... because it's ALL good stuff!

Learning to play the guitar is a progressive act. You'll be doing yourself a favor to take your time and let each day's material soak in so you have a really good understanding before moving on to the next.

We've got a lot to cover today, so let's get rockin'!

Parts of the Guitar

Before I get down to the nitty-gritty of learning how to play this weird piece of wood with a bunch of tight wires on it, it's probably a good idea to identify and understand what the various parts are called, how to properly hold it, and also how to hold what's called a guitar pick.

The guitar can be divided into three distinct parts:

- The main body
- The neck
- The headstock

No matter what kind of guitar you have (steel string acoustic, nylon string classical, or electric), you'll have these three main parts. Let's take a closer look and see what their actual functions are:

The Body

The body of the guitar is where the sound will come from. On an acoustic the strings make the top of the body (called the soundboard) vibrate, and the sound resonates naturally.

On an electric guitar, the sound comes through parts called "pickups" that translate the string vibrations into electrical signals that are then processed through a guitar amplifier.

The Neck

The neck is the long stick-like piece of wood that extends out from the guitar's body. Here is where you will take your fretting hand and will press down on the strings to change the notes that will ring out.

See those tiny bars of metal that are going up and down across the neck? Those are called frets, and you'll be putting your fingers in between them to make different notes off the same string.

Just a side note: if you are a right-handed player (in the vast majority) you will use your left hand to fret notes and your right hand to pick or strum the strings. Left-handed players use the right hand for fretting and the left hand to strum. *To keep any confusion down, in this book we will consider the left hand as the fretting hand and the right hand as the picking hand.*

The Headstock

The headstock is located at the top of the neck.

Take a look at the pictures below. See how each headstock has six separate parts — one for each string? Those are called "tuning machines", and the main purpose of a headstock is to give a place to mount them.

Time for a physics lesson. Don't freak out…this is actually kind of cool…

Tuning machines are what changes the amount of tension on a guitar string. When a tight string is plucked (either with your finger or a guitar pick) you will get a note. How that note sound is called the "pitch" of the note.

By tightening the string, the pitch will be higher. And if you loosen the string? You got it — the pitch gets lower. This is very important as it is a primary function of how a guitar works. There is a process called "tuning" where all of the strings are set to specific pitches so they sound well when played together properly. I'll be going into that whole process with you in a little bit.

How to Hold the Guitar

At first, holding a guitar will feel strange. Weird, actually. Take the time to do it correctly and it'll get to feel like a well-worn glove the second you sit down with it or strap it on when standing up.

The Proper Position

You'll want to place the guitar over your right leg, with your left hand holding and supporting the neck. Your right hand should be positioned over the sound hole on an acoustic and over the pickups on an electric:

How high you hold the guitar in relation to your body is important. During these beginner stages, you'll want to find a comfortable position, particularly for your left wrist. Getting a feel for the "right" position is important as it can be critical as your playing skills progress. Doing it wrong can lead to difficulty when trying to reach for certain notes relative to your hand position.

The ideal position is when your left hand is at a 90° with your left forearm. For now, you want to avoid placing your thumb over the neck. Place it slightly behind for the best positioning. Take a look below: the first picture shows the best way, and the one below it shows you what not to do:

Yup! You got it!   *Nope! Forget about it...*

As far as your right arm and hand are concerned, the best position will be different depending on the kind of guitar you are playing (acoustic vs. electric). Don't worry too much about that for now — just make sure that you can comfortably reach all of the strings.

Here's another tip: you'll want to avoid holding the guitar at an angle from your body. The proper position is to have the guitar run parallel to your torso, with the entire guitar body in contact with it. Holding it in the wrong way we just described is a very common mistake that beginners make, and it can force your hands into uncomfortable positions — especially if you are holding your hands and arms wrong for extended periods of time.

Check this out:

Got it again — you're a rock star!!   *Ummmm....nope. Try again!*

See how your arms and wrist are more in a straight line in the first picture? That's the right way to do it. You can see from the second picture how holding your guitar at the wrong angle can curve your arm into an uncomfortable position.

The Great Sit-Down-Stand-up Debate

Some sit down while playing…and some stand up. Does it matter?

Not really.

Well… it depends.

Sitting is common with acoustic players. I'm not saying that all of them sit, but you tend to see it more often. Some electric players sit as well, actually.

If you are a "sitter", then I'd suggest that you find a comfortable armless chair to practice in. Make sure that you can sit up so your back can be held in a straight position. Sitting in the wrong position can lead to back and shoulder strain…now who would want that?!?

Other players stand up. That's more typical of electric players and those that play on stage at gigs. You may encounter some back and shoulder discomfort at first because your body won't be used to holding a weight like that, even though guitars are relatively light. It'll go away the more you get used to it, though.

One point to keep in mind: there can be a difference in playing sitting down vs. standing up. Your entire body is in relatively different positions. Some songs that you'll be able to play while sitting may be hard to do so when standing up, and vice versa. Sometimes it may be best to just pick one over the other and always try to practice in that manner as much as possible.

How to Hold a Pick

Have you ever been on the main floor at a concert, and that awesome guitarist you are drooling over flicks out a few small, triangular shaped "things" into the crowd?

Those things are the lowly guitar pick. I say "lowly" because it's typically just a little piece of plastic. Without them, though, most guitar players would cease to exist!

Yeah, I'm exaggerating. Gotta have a little fun sometimes... life is too short to be boring!

Holding a guitar pick in the right way is crucial to playing correctly. The pick is to be held between your thumb and index finger on your right hand. It should be parallel to the line of your arm, with the sharp, pointy end pointing towards the strings, and you should typically hold it as close to the strings as possible.

Here are a few examples:

How the pick and your hand should look as you start to strum.

How the pick and your hand should look as you finish strumming.

The pick is too far to the left — bad technique.

The tip of the pick is lined up to the center — perfect technique.

The pick is too far to the right, you can hardly see it — bad technique.

Although these concepts are pretty simple and basic, you can't underestimate how important they are. Doing it wrong will make the guitar harder to play, and you can also develop bad habits that may take a long time for you to break. Just Say No and do it right from the beginning!

It certainly won't hurt to come back and review these points every now and then until you "get it", particularly if something feels wrong or if there's a position where your fingers just can't seem to reach.

How to Tune Your Guitar

Guitars, just like any other stringed instrument, need to go through a process called "tuning". Tuning is a simple process where you get the strings of your guitar to sound out specific notes when you play them open. This series of notes is called "standard tuning".

Standard tuning is setting up the strings to play the following open notes:

- 6th (thickest) string: E
- 5th string: A
- 4th string: D
- 3rd string: G
- 2nd string: B
- 1st (thinnest) string: E

Eddie **A**te **D**ynamite **G**ood-**B**ye **E**ddie — a good phrase to help remember the string names.

Using an Electronic Tuner

There are several methods that can be used to properly tune a guitar, but at first, I'll be looking at what is (by far) the easiest and most accurate, especially for a beginner - using an electronic tuner.

All electronic tuners work essentially in the same way. They measure the sonic frequency of a note as it rings out, and there is a small display on the tuner itself that will tell you what that note is.

If your string is "out of tune", then the tuner will tell you if you are flat (lower pitch) or sharp (higher pitch). You then adjust the tuning machine to add or take away tension so that the note will be perfectly referenced to the right frequency. Most (if not all) tuners will let you know when the note is correct, either by changing colors or having some sort of indicator that flashes.

Time to Take Some Notes...

One of the great things (if not the greatest) about using an electronic tuner is the fact that you only need to remember six notes: E, A, D, G, B, and E. You don't need to know anything else as far as how notes are related to the guitar, and all you really have to do is turn your tuning machines to get things spot-on.

Yes, you can tune your guitar manually, without the use of a tuner. It is much more of an involved process, and it's not necessarily what I'd recommend for a beginner. The fact of the matter is that there will be times where you might not have an electronic tuner available (like when the batteries go dead...ask me how I know).

In these cases, it really helps to know how to use fretted notes to tune. Yeah, it helps to have a little knowledge about notes and basic music theory here, but right now it's more important that you dig in and learn "how" to do it. The "why" will come to you later...trust me.

Manual Tuning

(Feel free to skip this subheading if it is too much to digest — you can come back to it later.)

As we discussed earlier, the guitar is tuned from the 6th string to the 1st string as E — A — D — G — B — E. The 6th string is the thickest one, and the 1st string is the thinnest one.

Like we said, tuning manually (also called tuning "by ear") *is not recommended for a beginner.* It really is an important skill you should take the time to develop, though. Let's take a look at how to do it, just as a point of reference.

To tune your guitar properly you have to compare fretted notes on one string to another string that is being played open.

Here's the tricky part — at first it can be hard to tell if two notes sound exactly the same or not. You may think so, but it's pretty easy when you're a beginner to not tell the difference very well. The more you play you'll find that your "ear" (or being able to sense the "correctness" of a note) will get better over time.

Take a look at the diagram below:

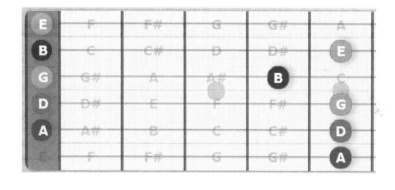

- ✓ 5th fret of the 6th string should be the same note as the open 5th string.

- ✓ 5th fret of the 5th string should be the same note as the open 4th string.

- ✓ 5th fret of the 4th string should be the same note as the open 3rd string.

- ✓ 4th fret of the 3rd string should be the same note as the open 2nd string.

- ✓ 5th fret of the 2nd string should be the same note as the open 1st string.

Notice anything special? These are the same notes you need to tune in standard tuning! So, in essence, we fret every note as described and compared with the next open note. Give it a try!

To tune the guitar, as shown above, it's assumed that the low E string (6th string) is tuned properly before you start out. That is, it is already set to voice a true E note. You must get an external reference of the E note from somewhere, and that's yet another reason why using an electronic tuner (or even one of the many free mobile apps out there) is really the best way to go — the reference is already built into the tuner. It saves a lot of effort and gets the results much faster than trying to "hear" the differences between the notes, especially when you are just starting out and your "ear" isn't developed yet.

Using the tuning machines

Let's take a minute and figure out how to adjust the tuning machines of the guitar.

Let's say that we are using an electronic tuner, for simplicity. And that our sixth string shows D# instead of E. Looking at the order of the notes, you'll notice that D# comes right before E. So, your string is tuned lower than the note it's supposed to be.

You'll need to slowly tighten the string by moving the tuner in a counter-clockwise motion. In order to do this in a controlled manner, we play the open string, and we start moving the tuner of the guitar as the string is making a sound. The electronic tuner will react to this change and show in real time the tuning of the string as you tighten it. Stop turning as soon as the display on the tuner shows that it is dead set on E (for this example).

Usually, it is easier to approach a note from below than loosening a string to a target note. The tuning will tend to be much more stable as the tension will tend to stay consistent as it is brought up to pitch, rather than brought down.

Tuning is a necessary evil, for sure. You simply can't play properly if the notes aren't in the right relationship to each other. You'll get to the point where your ear will tell you if things just don't sound as they normally do. When that happens, you're most likely out of tune.

Also, think about if you go into playing with other musicians in a live environment. All instruments — guitar, bass, and keyboards — need to be properly tuned with each other in order for things to not sound like fingernails down a chalkboard (makes my spine tingle just thinking about it) ...

OK — so you've now got a grip on how to tune your guitar. Now it's time to move on to playing some melodies (series of single notes).

Your First Melody

Yeah, yeah... I know...you want to get to the good stuff. I don't blame you! I'll give you credit for your enthusiasm, that's for sure.

But - the last thing that I'm going to do is set you up for being disappointed. No matter what, there are some basic things about playing the guitar that you really need to understand before you plow into things. That's a good thing, though. The more you know about these details up front then the better you will do right from the start. That's very important!

Sound like a deal? Well OK then... let's get things moving!

How to Fret a Note

Staring out we are going to look at playing single notes. That is where you take one of the fingers on your fretting hand and press down on one string, then use your pick to pluck the string.

Getting a grip on how to do this right can't be overlooked. You'll definitely be setting yourself back and keeping yourself from progressing if you can't fret and play a note cleanly so it rings out without sounding muffled.

There are a few things that you need to do when fretting a note. First off, the tip of your finger should be in contact with the string, pressing down on the fretboard. Be careful to use just the right amount of finger pressure, though. Too much will make the note sound slightly sharp (higher in pitch than it is supposed to), *and it's going to hurt!* On the flip side, too little pressure won't let the string vibrate as it should. You'll know if you aren't giving it enough if the note sounds "plunky".

"Plunky"... is that even a word? Well, it is now. Why? Because I said so. It's my book and I can write whatever I want.

It's the Guitar Head's world and I'm just letting everyone else live in it! :)

A Golden Nugget

Let's take a little detour for a minute, here. Sometimes you'll see that I don't really take this stuff all that seriously. Why? Because you can't! It's just playing guitar, and playing guitar is ultimately all about having fun and enjoying yourself. Keep things on the lighter side and you'll have a much better attitude towards learning. Keeping things fun will help keep you motivated and make you want to learn. Not a thing wrong with that!

Your guitar journey will be a million times easier if you get this simple principle down.

OK — now that we've got THAT little tidbit out of the way...

When fretting a single note, you should always use the tips of your fingers, not the fleshy part where your fingerprint is. The tips are where the finger can concentrate all of the pressure, and it'll give you some "mechanical advantage".

So, what's right and what's wrong? Take a look at these two pictures and see if you can tell:

Which one is right?

If you said the first picture, then you win! Using the tip of your finger all of your strength is concentrated on that one point — which is where it should be.

If you said the second picture, then... well... you might have to stay after class and write "I only fret notes with the tips of my fingers" one bajillion times on the blackboard. Here the finger strength is not being directed in the right place. This will require much more strength to get a clean sound. It's just bad form. Don't let yourself get into a bad habit — do it right from the get-go and your guitar-playing life will be much easier, for sure.

One other thing to note (no pun intended), with your finger positioned as it is in the second picture, you may find it hard to keep from blocking any adjacent strings from ringing out in the case where you may want to play two strings at the same time (more on that later).

A key ingredient in being able to fret a note like we just discussed is your thumb. It should be positioned right behind the fretboard, ideally around the center of the neck if at all possible. That allows you to create a "clamp" with your fingers, and it will greatly increase the amount of finger strength that you will have available.

Here's what your right-hand thumb and fingers should look like, and also an example of what not to do:

Oh Yeah!!

Oh No...

Where Do I Fret?

The final ingredient of the equation is where on the neck you actually place your finger. When fretting a note, you must always place your finger between the frets — never directly on them.

When playing a note at, for example, the first fret, your finger will actually be behind the fret. The pictures below show both the right and wrong way to play a note on the 6th string at the 1st fret:

It's important to always play as close to the fret as possible, as shown in the first picture. This is more critical when playing on the lower frets that are farther apart. As you go up the neck, the frets get so close together that it really doesn't matter that much, as long as you keep your finger off the actual fret.

Play around with it. At this point it doesn't really matter where you are

Yup! *Nope!*

playing the notes — what's important is that your technique is correct. Play notes all over the neck, from the 6th string on the 1st fret all the way up to the highest note on the 1st string — and everywhere in between. You'll come to see that the position of your fretting hand may have to change a bit depending on where you are. That's perfectly OK because that's what you need to do to get the notes to ring out properly.

Now that you know how to play a note properly, let's get into the good stuff — actually making music and playing your first melody. We've got one little pitstop to make though…there is a special way to write down melodies so we need to take a look at how it's done.

Guitar Tablature — What It Is and How to Use It

Let's clear up something right out of the box:

> *"To learn to play the guitar, you do NOT have to learn how to read sheet music."*

Yep. That's right.

There are many famous guitarists that do not know how to read formal music. Notable mentions are The Beatles, Eric Clapton, and Eddie Van Halen. To be clear, though, I am NOT saying that learning to read music is a bad thing. Quite the contrary. But it IS true that you may be able to reach your guitar-playing goals without having to figure out how to read pages upon pages of black lines with what looks like squashed ants all over the page.

To make things easier (MUCH easier), let's talk about an alternative way of noting (no pun intended...again) how to play the guitar. It's called "guitar tablature", or "tab" for short. It is somewhat similar to formal sheet music but it is much easier to understand, especially for beginner guitarists.

It looks like this (hint ...here's your very first melody):

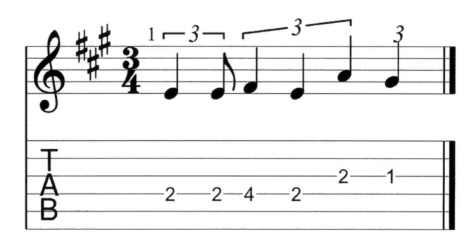

Melody 1

The part on the top represents formal music notation. No need to concern yourself with that now; in fact, many times when you see guitar tab the music notation isn't there at all. It is a good resource if you ever decide to take on learning how to read proper sheet music.

OK, so let's take a real good look at the lower section — the one that says "TAB" on it. You'll see that there are six lines that run horizontally across the page. Each line represents one string of your guitar, with the line at the bottom representing the 6th string, and the line at the top representing the 1st string. Simple enough, right?

Therefore, when the guitar is on your lap, the string closest to you on the guitar (the 6th or Low (Thickest) E string) is the line closest to you on the TAB. And the string furthest from you on the guitar (the 1st or High (Thinnest) E string) is the line furthest away from you on the TAB. Some people do find this confusing at first, but it gets very easy, very quickly with a little practice.

The numbers represent the frets that you are supposed to play the notes on. Even more simple!

There are other elements of the reading tab that are similar to music notation, such as time signatures and measures. No need to go into that now - let's just concentrate on getting the notes right.

Let's check it out the tab again:

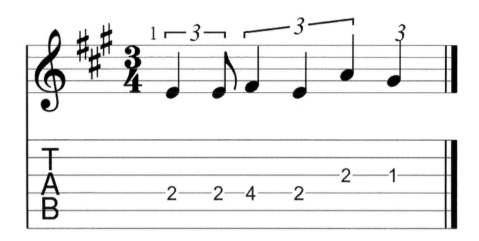

Melody 1

If you read the tab correctly, you'll play the following notes one after the other. Try using the fingers I have noted to help develop your fretting hand strength and dexterity.

- ✓ 4th string — 2nd fret (index)
- ✓ 4th string — 2nd fret (index)
- ✓ 4th string — 4th fret (ring)
- ✓ 4th string — 2nd fret (index)
- ✓ 3rd string — 2nd fret (index)
- ✓ 3rd string — 1st fret (index)

Looking at the diagram below, you'll see that each finger on your fret hand can be related to a number:

As you become more accustomed to working with guitar tabs you'll sometimes see where certain fingers are recommended to play certain notes (as we did above). Tab will relate to the fingers as the numbers shown.

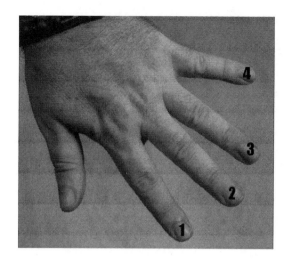

- Index finger = 1
- Middle finger = 2
- Ring finger = 3
- Pinky finger = 4

Always try to use any song or exercise as an opportunity to work on your fretting hand. You simply can't use just one finger to play the guitar correctly — you need to learn to use all four.

A simple way to envision this is to picture a four-fret "box", with each fret being played by one finger. This will allow you, as your skills progress, to change positions smoothly and have a good frame of reference for which fingers should play which notes based on your hand position.

Once you have a good understanding of how to position your hand, practice the melody over and over, taking it slow and easy. You can even check out the audio tracks so you can hear exactly how it is supposed to sound.

Now that you've played it (and maybe even listened to the audio)... does it ring a bell? Sounds like "Happy Birthday" to me — and it will to you too after you get it down pat!

This book comes with audio tracks for all the charts. You should check out the bonus section at the start of the book if you don't have it yet.

Muscle Memory

One important facet of guitar playing is developing what is called "muscle memory".

Generally, once you figure out which finger to use for each note on a melody, you should try to stick to that fingering pattern for as you practice. And practice you should - over and over, time and time again. This helps you to memorize it because it develops muscle memory. That is the best way to learn stuff on the guitar. You play something until your fingers go on autopilot. You'll be surprised at how things may get better each time you do it.

At first, it will seem impossible, but trust me, it happens. You don't need to think "left foot on the floor, raise right knee, move the right leg forward, place right foot on the floor" and so on when you walk, right? You just do it automatically; your muscle memory takes care of it. The same thing happens with the fingers when you make a lot of repetitions.

Hey, Arnold Schwarzenegger didn't get to look like he did in his heyday without doing a lot (and I mean a LOT) of reps with his weights. In the same light, you won't be able to play like Jimmy Page without doing a bunch of reps on your own!

Bringing Day 1 to a Close...

Whew...

Congratulations! You just made it through a pretty long day! I can imagine that you may be experiencing some mental overload...but that's to be expected. Taking on something new like learning to play the guitar is a challenge that few take...and even fewer succeed at. Something tells me you're going to be one of the ones that break on through to the other side...

I mean, seriously! Look at everything that you've learned in just one day!

- ✓ Parts of the guitar
- ✓ How to hold your guitar

- ✓ How to hold a guitar pick
- ✓ How to tune your guitar
- ✓ You played your first melody
- ✓ How to read guitar tab

I'll tell you what — I'm impressed!

Take a break for now and let's hit it back up tomorrow — you've definitely earned it.

DAY 2

More Melodies...

Yeah, I know. Playing the same line over...and over...and over again can become a bit boring. So why not mix it up a bit? There's no hard and fast rule that says you have to completely master one thing before moving on to another.

Actually, sometimes that is a better way to approach your practicing. Boredom can become your enemy as far as guitar playing goes. Keep it fresh by taking on a few more things – but take care to not overload yourself. That can be an even worse enemy than boredom!

Here are a few more for you to work on:

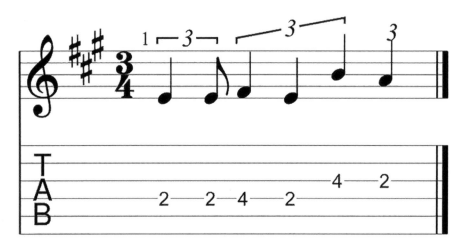

Melody #1

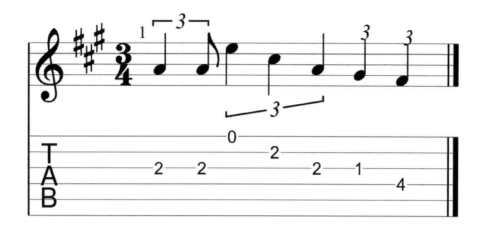

Melody #2

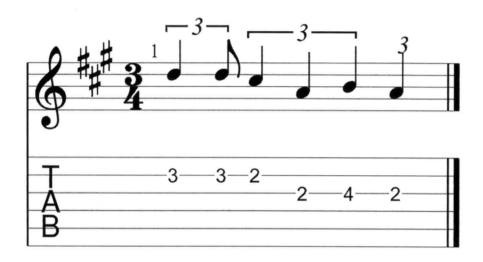

Melody #3

So, how do you know if you're getting it right? Check out the audio tracks that are included.

As with all of the melodies we have looked at, my advice to you is the same — start off slow, make sure the notes are sounding as they should, and then you can build up your speed as you get better.

And here's a little secret that I purposely left out — when you play all of these melodies one after another, you'll end up with the complete melody for Happy Birthday.

> **BONUS UPDATE:** *I have 6 more melodies for you! You thought I was going to leave you with only one, didn't you? These ones are fancier and come with backing tracks you can play along with — check the section at the end of this chapter for it.*

How much should I practice?

Another Golden Nugget

This is the perfect context to discuss an important mindset shift. This section was designed as the introduction to the book but it would make a lot more sense after you have spent a little time with the guitar.

Do you know *practice* is the biggest reason people give up on guitar? Yup, you read that right! To make it clearer — over-practicing or being a perfectionist with guitar is the biggest reason you see so many unused guitars lying around in people's attics. This is a common problem among guitarists — even the seasoned ones. I've lost many years of progress to my perfectionist syndrome.

Let's bring up a story to better explain the perfectionist syndrome — James was a beginner and was learning his first melody. He got the melody "more or less" right and moved on to exercises and chords. He knew he hadn't got his melody perfect to the dot, but James was in for the fun of playing guitar and not to play better than the artist who created the melody.

He did the same with chord too — he wasn't perfect at it, but he did his best and started playing his first few songs. There were a few missed strums and "plunky" sounds in his playing, but he loved the progress he was making and moved onto scales and soloing.

He made so much progress in his first few months that when he came back to his first melody — he could play it with eyes closed and even improvise to give the melody his own "flavor".

Now, imagine if James was stuck on getting his first melody right and making sure everything sounds perfect — it would've taken him months to even start the next lesson! He most probably would've quit in frustration even before giving his first song a shot.

You see, as you progress through your guitar journey — you start getting good! Muscle memory takes over and you can start playing without even thinking about it! Your goal as a beginner is not to get all the songs perfect — but to train those muscles to take over your playing and make things *automatic*.

You can always come back to these melodies once you've covered some ground to perfect it and beat Beethoven at his symphonies.

Why 7 days

This whole book has been created around this simple concept. This is the reason I give you a day by day schedule to follow and goals to hit. To make sure you are only practicing "enough" and not over doing it. There's no way you can get through all the exercises and melodies of day 2 while over-practicing. Pretty clever eh?

I know that some people need more time than the others — if you're someone who needs a little more time — I've made sure to include an *extended timeline* for certain sections. But make sure you don't cross the extended timeline — this means you're simply over-practicing.

That was a long detour — let's get back to our topic at hand now.......

Finger Exercises

As you can see, you can turn songs into exercises. That's the fun part!

Sorry to take things down a notch, but sometimes — especially when you are just starting out — playing songs and familiar melodies won't give you all of the basic techniques that you'll need to develop in order to advance your playing skills.

For this section, we are going to tackle some standard finger exercises that are designed to increase your finger dexterity and muscle memory. Granted, these may not be as fun as playing an actual song, but they are important to help fill in the gaps for proper techniques. You need to have a solid foundation to build your skill sets from, so it's never a bad thing to keep these in your back pocket to practice when you get the chance.

Here's the key for working on finger exercises — they aren't necessarily meant to sound cool or melodic. They are intended to build up your skills. So what if you don't get it right the first time? Or the second…or the tenth? These are *exercises* — and repetition is key to developing the right skills.

Exercise 1

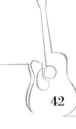

Exercise 2

Exercise 3

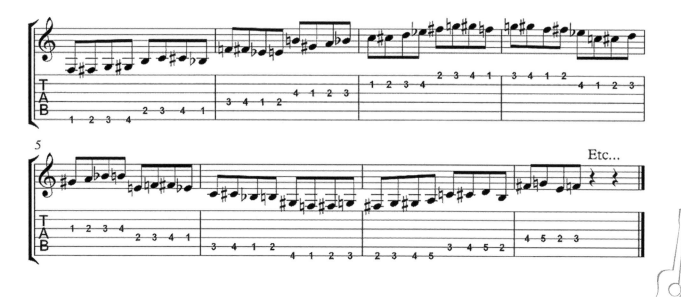

> **EXTENDED DEADLINE:** *You may take an extra day to nail the exercises, if required. But if it takes you more than that — you are being a perfectionist.*

Sore fingers?

If you've been practicing the melodies and exercises for some time, it's a pretty safe bet that you have inevitably ended up with sore fingers. This is completely normal for every guitarist and it's nothing to get discouraged about.

As you practice, you'll start building calluses on your fingertips. This should protect you from the strings. But that takes time, and you need to be patient with it.

A quick warning, if your fingers get too sore to play — *you need to take a break*! I know you're excited to learn but the last thing you want is a blister on your finger that can take weeks to heal.

Well...I think that's a pretty good introduction to the fundamentals of fretting notes, reading guitar tab, and playing single note melodies. It's time to start considering what happens when you play more than one string at a time.

Bringing Day 2 to a Close...

I think you're getting your groove on, here.

Not only did you learn a bunch of new melodies, but we also took a good look at a bunch of finger exercises that are great for developing the dexterity on your fretting hand.

Doesn't seem like much, maybe, but today is my payback for all of the stuff that you took in on Day 1. Avoiding terminal mental overload is a good thing, trust me.

So, what do you think? Are you ready (and willing) for Day 3?

Bonus Melodies

This section is an update to the book after its initial debut. It was after I released the book that I realized I don't have enough variety in melodies. Not everyone wants to play the Happy Birthday tune. Hence, I added this section in.

This part is a bonus section and will put you off track towards your 7-day goal. Hence, I recommend coming back to it after the 7 days or you can take an extra day or two to cover it if you're not in a rush.

I decided to go overboard with this part of the book and created videos and backing tracks for you to follow along. The tabs to the melodies are given below. You'll find the backing tracks and audio versions of these melodies in the bonus section of the book.

And if you want to check out the videos, you can follow this link:

http://bit.ly/songs-melodies

The above will take you to a YouTube playlist with all the videos of this book. This way is much simpler than having to download those big files.

(If you're wondering, a backing track is exactly what it says. You put the track in the back and play along with it. It'll make it sound like you're playing with an entire band! It's pretty fun, you should check it out.)

Beginner Melody 1

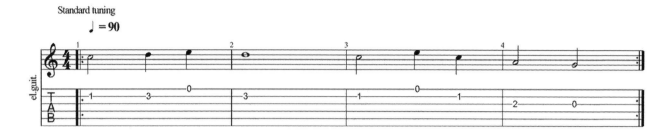

Beginner Melody 2

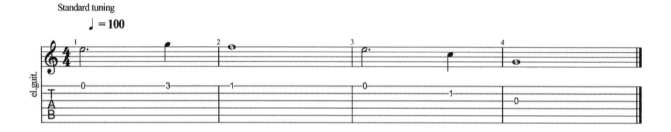

Beginner Melody 3

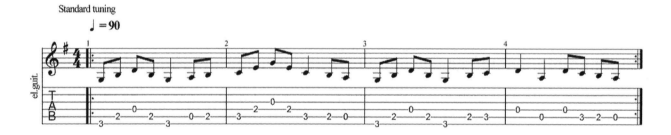

Beginner Melody 4

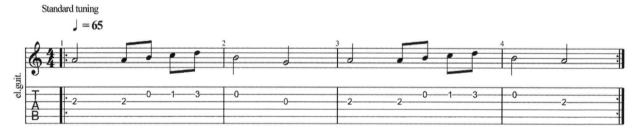

Beginner Melody 5

Beginner Melody 6

DAY 3

Your First Chords

Welcome to Day 3!

Today is a big day for you... because it's the day you will learn to play your first chords!

Being able to play the guitar is a lot more than just playing single note lines and melodies. I mean, think about it... how many songs have you heard where it was just notes and nothing else?

"Chords" is a general term used when you play three or more strings at the same time while fretting certain notes. Confused? Yeah, I know... but it's really not as bad as you may think.

To keep things simple (I've been saying that a lot, I know... but simple is better when you're first starting out), we are going to learn just three chords. Why only three? Because that's all you need to play a *ton* of songs using very simple sequences. Remember, the idea is to get you playing music as fast as possible, right?

The chords we are going to work on are called:

A major, D major, and E major.

Just so that you know, chords can be either "major" or "minor". Where we're at right now, all you need to know is that major chords sound happy and minor chords sound sad. It is a mix of both that can give a song its "feel".

One thing to point out — try to not get the chord names confused with note names. For example, there is a D chord and a D note. The difference is that with a chord there are several different notes played together, whereas a note is only a single sound.

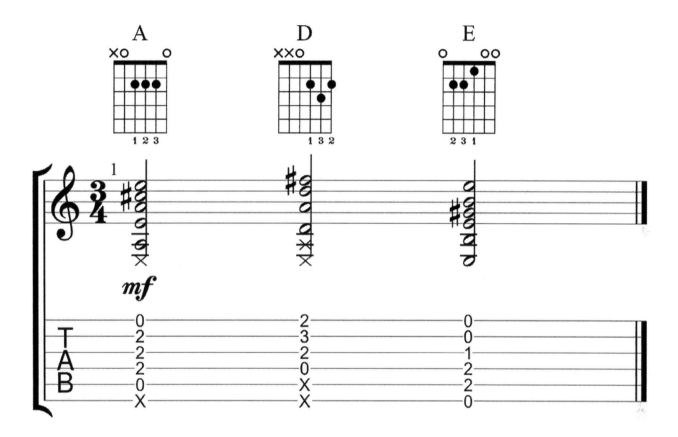

Here's some guitar tab with the chords we are going to learn:

(An audio track which plays the above 3 chords in the same order is available — give it a listen to understand how the chords should sound)

Another way that you'll see chords written out is in chord diagrams. These simple diagrams show you how to play the chords in a more graphic form, with the frets numbered, as well as the finger we are supposed to use for each note. Each horizontal line represents a fret, each vertical line a string,

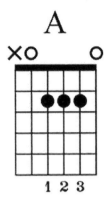
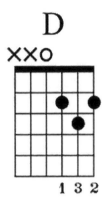
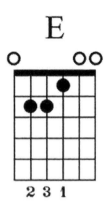

and each circle shows the note which finger you should use to play it.

When you just write the main note (a.k.a. the root note), it's commonly understood that you are talking about a major chord. For example, seeing a simple "E" in a chord diagram would mean the E major chord, and a "D" would mean the D major chord. Let's practice each chord individually first so that you can get your fingers in exactly the right places.

I'd suggest starting out with the nice and easy A Major (A). Then you can continue with D major, (D) and then the E major (E).

A major (A)　　　　　*D Major (D)*　　　　　*E major (E)*

This is what they look like once they are placed on the instrument:

Once you get familiar with these chords, you'll need to play them in a sequence, or a specific order (commonly called a "chord progression"). The sequence we are going to play is a very common one that is used in lots of popular songs (a list of some of the songs you can play with these chords is located at the end of Day 7).

To play the chords, the only thing we need to do is to sweep our pick through the strings, playing them all in the same stroke. This is called a "strum".

Things to watch out for

Getting all the notes to sound nice and clear when you play any of these chords is very difficult at first. Don't rush and be patient. Concentrate on getting every note to produce an un-muffled sound. Move your finger and press harder on each note until you get it to sound good. You may also need to move your other fingers which may be touching the string your playing and giving it a dead sound. This is particularly common with the D chord and A chord.

Once you've played the notes individually and they all sound good or at least OK, then strum the whole chord. This is very important because you learn to press all your fingers down together at the same time. Then move on to another chord and go through the whole process again.

As a side note here, it's really, REALLY important that you don't let yourself get frustrated. Playing chords at first can be tough. Rarely will a beginner get it right the first time out — I'm just being honest.

It's a challenge, but practice makes perfect, right? So, let's also take a look at some things that commonly can go wrong, because if you know what to look for you'll be able to get things sounding a lot clearer in much less time.

The first time you tried the chord, you probably got a "plunky" (it's a real word now, remember?) sound rather than a clear chord sound. Your fingers are probably touching everywhere except where they are supposed to, and most of the notes are getting muted.

The first question that might come to a beginner's mind is: "Are my fingers too fat?"

Don't laugh — I have honestly heard many people say this...

Nope — your fingers are absolutely fine! You're just not holding the chord right.

Playing chords requires you to hold the guitar the correct way. You might get away with sloppy posture if you're playing single string tunes. But chords? No way.

As we discussed on Day 1, you should be pressing on the strings with the absolute tip of your fingers, and they should be perpendicular to the fretboard. Also, try curling your palm inwards to get a better grip around the neck.

This part is all about trial and error until you find the sweet spot. Hold the chord, try picking each string individually to see if they ring properly. If they don't ring out, you need to adjust whichever finger is causing the problem a little. When they do ring out, try to remember that hand position.

It's important to realize that what may be the "perfect" hand position for one chord may not be for another one. Just as the fingering patterns for each chord are different, so is the way you have to hold your hand to get things comfortable and with the proper form.

Take your time with this — you aren't on a schedule. It's like good barbecue — low and slow will give you the best results...

Great. Now I'm hungry...

Once you feel you've gotten all three chords down, we can move on to bigger and better things. Playing chords correctly is great, but it really doesn't mean jack squat unless you string them together to play a song.

Bringing Day 3 to a Close...

You really can't underestimate what you've learned today.

Think about it for a minute. Consider every song that you have ever heard (no, I'm not exaggerating). Everyone that has ever been written is comprised of chords, and you'll be amazed by how many of them are made up of A, D, and E.

Many guitarists when they first start out don't realize that fact. They hear someone playing a killer guitar solo and think that *that's* what true guitar playing is all about.

But, no it isn't. Not by a long shot. 99% of a song is how it's been constructed. Chords are the cake of a song, and the solos are just the icing on top.

Until tomorrow... we'll meet again...!

DAYS 4 & 5

Mastering Chord Shifting

Congratulations!

Learning to play some common chords is a big accomplishment. Now that you've done that on Day 3 and are familiar with them, you and I need to look at how to string them together to produce one solid musical statement.

Learning how to play an individual chord is impressive, but it takes on an entirely different meaning when you play them together.

Then it really means something – not just to you but also to the people that are listening to you play (and getting better every day, I might add...).

That's why Day 4 and Day 5 are both going to be spent on one topic – learning how to shift between chords. It's one of the most important skills for any guitar player to have because you simply can't play songs without truly knowing how to do it.

So, without further ado...

Mastering the Shift

Playing chords, and doing it right, is something to be proud of. What will make you even more impressed with your fine self is when you string (no pun intended, for the hundredth time) them together to create a chord progression.

The magic chord progression that I've been referring to is one that a lot of songs use. I think you'll actually be pretty surprised as to how many songs you'll be able to play once you get it nailed. The chord progression is as follows: A – D — E — A (which reads as A major, D major, E major, A major).

Taking your playing to the next level means being able to quickly and smoothly shift between chords. Like most things with the guitar, it may seem a little awkward at first. Keep at it and you'll end up being able to switch chords like a pro!

I've got three tips for you to make things a little easier. Everyone can use a little help from their friends, right?

Right!

Anticipate

The first important rule is to try to stay ahead of the curve. When you're playing a chord and you can already hear that it sounds correct, you should immediately start thinking of the next chord in the progression. Trying to visualize it on the fretboard before you shift to the chord is a great mental exercise.

Really, all musicians play like this, from the bedroom beginner to the established professional. What you hear has already been processed in their minds, and they are always thinking of their next chord.

Minimize movement

This second tip will make you ultra-efficient when it comes to moving your fingers. One thing that most beginners tend to do is "clear" the fretboard as they are going from one chord to the next, completely removing the entire hand and fingers from the neck.

Think about that though — the more distance you put between the fretboard and your fingers, the more distance you'll need to move to get back to it for the next chord, right? It's a fraction of a second that we are talking here, but it is enough to make the music we play sound sloppy. So, always strive to keep your fingers as close to the fretboard as possible.

Slide into it!

Placing three different fingers in different places on the fretboard at the same time is difficult when you first start doing it - if only there was a simpler way? Well, there is! By sliding into chords.

Let's take the change from an E chord to a D chord for example. First of all, play an E chord. You will notice that your first finger is on the third string (G) on the first fret. Now, lift your send and third fingers off the fretboard, but leave the first finger where it is.

Then slide the first finger up to the second fret, then put your second finger on the first string (E) on the second fret and add your third finger on the second string (B) on the third fret. And you've got a D chord! So give it a strum and give yourself a pat on the back. But, this is quite difficult, especially with a guitar on your lap, so probably best to not bother with that.

Anyway... now, lift the second and third fingers, leaving the first finger in place, then slide the first finger back to the first fret and put the other two fingers down to make an E chord again. Repeat this change until it becomes easy.

The note that slides between the chords acts as an anchor, so your other fingers know what they have to do and where they have to go. This is one of the biggest secrets to playing your first song in only 7 days, but you can use the technique through all your years of playing.

D to A to D to A etc.

The same thing applies to changing from a D to an A, but this time the third finger is the anchor. So, play the D chord as normal, then lift the first and second fingers off but leave the third finger where it is. Now slide the third finger back one fret and put your other two fingers above it on the fretboard and you've got an A chord. So give it a strum!

Next, take the first and second fingers back off, slide the third finger back up a fret and put the first and second fingers back on and you're back playing a D chord! Again repeat the change until it becomes second nature.

A to D to E to D to A

This must be getting a little confusing by now so I won't give a full explanation of how to do this chord progression using slides, but it's easy enough for you to work it out for yourself. Then practice it over and over until you play it like a pro!

BTW: there is no slide that will take you from an E chord to an A chord, so you will have to lift all three fingers for that chord change.

The 2 Chord Shift

In order to really nail this chord progression, you'll need to practice each chord combination separately. Start by playing A, and then play a D, remember to use the sliding technique. Then practice D, going to E, again remember to slide your first finger. Then E back to A. Make sure you isolate each shift and practice them until you can play each one with relative ease.

Once you've gotten "all shifty" and stuff, it's time to put everything together. Since we haven't really talked about strumming yet, let's keep it simple for now. Play a chord by striking all the strings with the pick in one motion (also known as "strumming", as we mentioned before), then count till 4 and change the chord.

Imagine counting 1-2-3-4 • 1-2-3-4…continuously in the same tempo. Now strum the A chord by playing all strings as you say 1, count, 2,3,4, change to D as you say 1 out loud, etc. Do this for the entire sequence and then start the progression again from the A chord.

Bringing Days 4 and 5 to a Close…

While the material for Days 4 & 5 may seem kind of short (page-wise in the book, anyway), I'm hoping that by now you can see how important it is to play a chord properly and then be able to shift to another one with relative ease.

And by "relative ease", I know that some of you may be thinking:

"Easy? Is he nuts?!?
I'm having a heck of a time getting this down!!"

But, get it down you will. Just keep at it. You've already learned more in five days than many people that think they want to play guitar ever learn. There are so many people that get frustrated, lose interest, and just let their guitars sit.

Guitars are meant to be played, folks!

And I know that you've got the motivation and determination to keep it going. Think about it — we have only two days left until you can say you are playing your first song!

<u>**Two short days.**</u>

Yeah… you got this.

Let's hit things back up tomorrow.

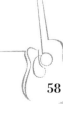

DAY 6

Playing with the Right Rhythm

Welcome to Day 6.

Just today and one more day to go before you've got it nailed!

So, now you can string chords together and shift from one to the other. It's time to take a look at how to do that with the right timing and rhythm…

Set the Beat

Have you ever found yourself tapping your foot or nodding your head to your favorite tune?

Congratulations — you just found the tempo of the song!

Everything in rhythm is related to the tempo of a song. For most music, the tempo determines the length of the most basic rhythmic figure, which is called a quarter note. This can also be referred to as the basic beat. Therefore, one tap of your foot equals one-quarter note or one beat.

In most songs, there are four beats to a bar. Now don't get excited, this has nothing to do with the place you go for a relaxing drink and a chat with your buddies. A bar of music is completely different from a bar that sells beer — unfortunately!

Anyway, back to the point... every bar contains four quarter notes which equal the four beats of the bar. So, if you tap your foot in rhythm to a song four times, you will more than likely be tapping out a whole bar.

Now a bar can be split in any number of ways, the four quarter notes we have just covered obviously being one of them, but these can also be subdivided to make eight 8th notes. On the other hand, the bar does not have to be split into four or eight notes, it could be split in two giving us two half notes.

This may all sound quite complicated, but, it's just simple math at the end of the day, one bar equals one whole beat, two half note beats, four quarter note beats or eight 8th note beats.

Here's a partial table with the figures that were just discussed, and a way to visualize how everything fits together.

How does all of this relate to the guitar? Well, we're going to use it to understand strumming, which means playing all of the strings at once.

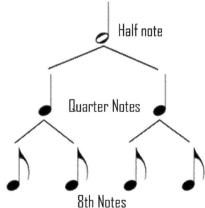

Other Time Signatures

But, four isn't the only number of beats that can be in a bar, to simplify things even further you can have three beats in a bar, i.e. 1, 2, 3 — 1, 2, 3 — etc. This is commonly known as Waltz Time because every Waltz is written in this time signature. It is represented as 3/4, as opposed to 4/4, or what is referred to as Common Time.

There are other time signatures as well, but they tend to be more complicated than 3/4 and 4/4, so will not be covered in this book.

Strumming

> **EXTENDED DEADLINE:** *If you need it, feel free to take an extra day to nail the strumming part. Again, don't be a perfectionist about it.*

First, play any of the three chords that you have learned. Now play all the 6 strings in just one downstroke (moving the pick down towards the floor). Now try to play all the 6 strings with an upstroke (moving the pick back up towards the ceiling). This movement is called strumming.

Strumming is an essential skill to master, regardless of what kind of guitar you play or the type of music you like to listen to and want to play. So, here are a few tips to keep you on the right path.

The strumming motion should come from the elbow — not the wrist. Your wrist should remain relaxed but should remain in line with your arm at all times as the arm moves up and down while playing. But, it shouldn't be stiff — so keep a relaxed wrist but minimize the movement; you don't want to be a robot!

In order to keep the strumming even and musical, do your best to keep your upstrokes and downstrokes at the same speed and apply the same amount of pressure as you play both. You will, of course, change this as you get better and start to play more intricate rhythm patterns.

Also, don't make a fist with your strumming hand, leave the fingers open, which will give you more control and not give you the heavy-handed feel of someone who is fighting their guitar, not working with it.

Here's a couple of pictures of what it should look like as the arm goes down and up.

After a downstroke *After an upstroke*

Now that we know the basics of the technique, it's time to learn a few rhythms. Here's a very simple one to get started. This is in 3/4 time.

Rhythm 1

A

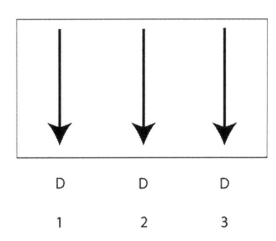

This is a simple one strum per beat rhythm, count 1, 2, 3 and strum downwards on every beat. 'D' signifies a 'downstroke'. And don't forget to check out the audio examples to hear exactly how it should sound.

Now we'll now add an upstroke. This occurs halfway between the second and third downstrokes, which gives us the pattern below.

Rhythm 2

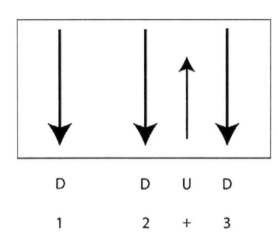

This can either be counted 1, 2+3 or D DUD. And did you notice that by simply adding a single upstroke, we get a far more interesting sounding rhythm which flows better and is much more usable within songs.

Now, we'll move on to some more rhythms, but in 4/4 time.

Rhythm 3

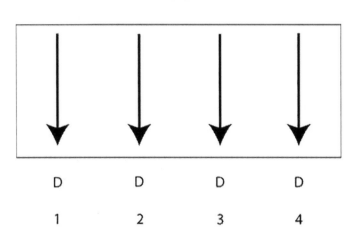

This is a simple one strum per beat rhythm similar to Rhythm 1, but this time count 1, 2, 3, 4 and strum downwards on every beat. The 'D' once again signifies a 'downstroke'. And remember that if you want to hear what it sounds like, then please check out the audio examples.

We'll now add an upstroke as we did for Rhythm Pattern 2. But, this one occurs halfway between the third and fourth downstrokes, which gives us.

Rhythm 4

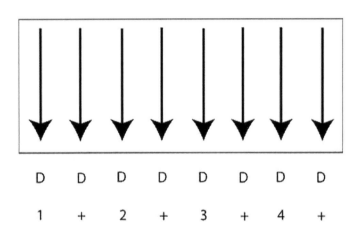

Again, as with Rhythm pattern 2, by simply adding a single upstroke, we get a far more interesting sounding rhythm. This can be counted as 1, 2, 3+4. Or as D, D, DUD. Again, refer to the audio examples to hear how this sounds and to make sure you're playing it correctly.

Rhythm 5

Alright — so now let's play 8 notes instead of 4, as shown in the diagram above. We'll set the same tempo as before (60-70 BPM) but the strums should occur twice as often. So, there will be TWO strums for every one beat. It might seem tricky to do, but you should keep the following in mind:

The key thing to focus on whenever music gets faster is to try and remain as relaxed as possible. Music, as in any Art, is an honest expression and if you're stressed or anxious, there's a good chance that you'll play that way. So, try and relax as much as you can, your playing will thank you for it.

Now that we've got those rhythms down, let's try a few more. We'll keep on naming each of them, just in case we need to refer to them later on. And to make it more realistic, we'll also include the chord or chords that you have to play while practicing these rhythms.

Rhythm 6

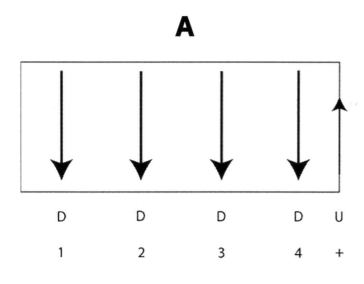

This is similar to the third rhythm we learned but with an additional upstroke played between the last strum of the bar and the first strum of the next bar.

As with all these rhythm patterns, listen to the audio examples to get a feel for what you should be playing and what it should sound like.

Rhythm 7

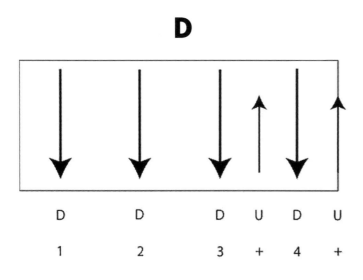

This is a combination of Rhythm 5 and Rhythm 6.

Understanding the metronome

Imagine you're running on a treadmill and your friend suddenly slows down the speed or even worse, makes the treadmill go faster! What was supposed to be a healthy way of keeping fit could suddenly turn into anything from a scene in a comedy to a mass of flying body!

It's pretty much the same when a musician is playing. The audience is enjoying every bit of it and suddenly the musician changes the speed (or tempo). Not keeping a solid tempo is a common mistake that many beginners make. Fortunately, learning to keep a consistent tempo is easy to practice if you use a handy little device called a metronome.

Consider a metronome as your timekeeper. You can easily download metronome apps, which are widely available for free, or you can grab a physical unit online or at your local music store.

The metronome usually shows a number followed by the BPM (Beats Per Minute). BPM is how we measure the speed of the tempo. The higher the BPM, the faster the tempo will be.

Let's set the metronome to around 60 to 70 BPM, and turn that sucker on. A sound will begin playing at regular intervals. These intervals are our quarter notes. Every time you hear that click or tick sound, you have to play the chord as notated in the diagram above. So, you should try to make every strum match the exact timing of each strike of the metronome. Make sense?

Chances are, you'll automatically start strumming in a downward direction for every quarter note and that's perfect. Congratulations! You're ready for your next challenge.

> **QUICK TIP:** *If you are playing in exact sync with the metronome, the sound of the metronome will be replaced with the sound of your guitar.*

Take a rest...

The final piece of the puzzle is the "rests". In music, the silence between the notes is just as important as the notes themselves. And, even though you're not playing anything when the rest appears, you normally still have to move your body to keep the groove going.

Basically, you still keep the movement going, as if you were actually strumming (moving your arm down or up), but not actually strum the strings. This helps maintain the tempo and a smooth rhythm.

A word of caution here: This will be difficult at first and you might feel silly doing it, but do it anyway. Stopping while you are learning to play a new rhythm, especially when you're first starting out, rarely sounds good. So, do your very best to just keep going, don't worry if it doesn't sound superb when you first start doing it and don't worry if it feels completely unnatural. Just persevere and remember that a good rhythmic foundation is the key to becoming a good musician.

Keep this in mind — solos are cool (REALLY cool), but the majority of a song is made up of chords that are played with a good rhythm and in perfect tempo. So yeah... this stuff might seem a little confusing at first, but it's very important that you spend time mastering it!

Bringing Day 6 to a Close...

So here we are — Day 6 has bitten the dust.

I've got a little secret for you-you're done!

Yep — that's right. You should now possess a good, solid knowledge of the basic skills needed to play your first song.

And that, my friend, is where Day 7 comes into play...

DAY 7

Your First Song

Day 7.

Wow... we're here already!

It really didn't take all that long now, did it?

Truthfully, it may have taken less time for some and maybe a bit longer for others, but that's OK. As long as you've learned what you can in a timeframe that's good for you, that's really all that matters.

Oh! — And one final thing before we start off with all your new songs — I want you to have a look at the end of this chapter when you are done. There's something I need your help with, but you'll need to have learnt your first song before you can do that.

Let's finally put the rubber to the road, because its —

Time for some real songs!!

Here are two songs written with their chords and strumming for you to practice:

First, let's begin with a song that uses Rhythm Pattern 2 throughout. That was the second one that you just learned on Day 6. So, here goes for a song that you will play at least once a year, but probably a lot more than that, for your lifetime!

Happy Birthday 3/4

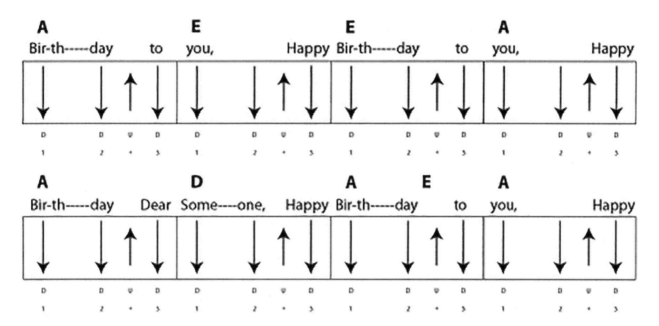

You will notice that the first word is 'Bir-th-----day', how can that be right? Well, it's because you actually sing the word 'Happy' before starting to play the first bar of the song. This is normally done by singing the word, then the guitar joins in for the second word — 'Birthday'. Or, if you prefer, you can play a few bars of an A chord at the beginning and then start singing 'Happy' at the end of one of them, before continuing with the rest of the song as shown above.

It's also a good idea to listen to the audio examples that accompany the book to make sure that you're playing the song properly.

And, if your wondering, why it's 'Bir-th-----day' and not 'Birthday', it's because you sing the different syllables of the word (as well as all other words) over the beats indicated by the downstrokes.

So, now that you're able to celebrate everyone's favorite day in style, let's move on to our next song, which is a little bit more of a handful, but not in the way your thinking…

He's Got the Whole World in his Hands 4/4

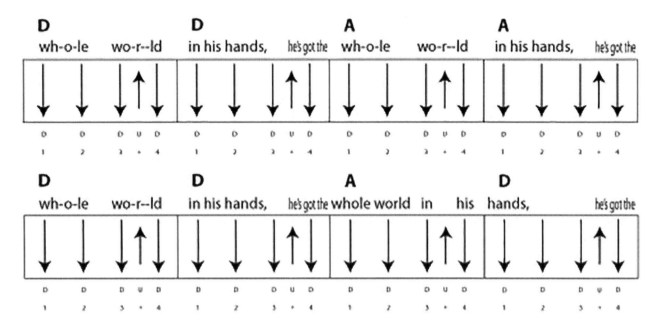

This song is in 4/4, therefore, we use rhythm pattern 4 throughout. And, as in Happy Birthday you either need to start singing "He's got the" before you start strumming the first D chord, or start the song by strumming D continually as an intro and then sing "He's got the" just before the chord progression starts.

But do you notice anything about these two songs?

Songs are basically just chords played in a certain order, at a certain tempo. That's really all there is to it!

I know, I know…you're thinking "that can't be it. This can't be that easy."

Oh, but it can. And it is!

Here's the exciting thing though — you can take the three chords that we have learned and play a ton of familiar and popular songs.

I actually wanted to include these songs in the book with chord charts etc., but those pesky publishers and copyright holders wouldn't let me do that. Well, they would, if I paid them lots of money, which would mean significantly increasing the cost of the book, which I really didn't want to do.

But, if you apply what you've learned already to these songs, you'll be playing most of them in no time at all. And remember, they all use the same three chords — A, D and E — and most use simple strumming patterns. The last few are a little harder, but by the time you get to them, you'll be ready to give them a go. And, since your developing so quickly as a guitarist now, we wanted to give you a few examples that would stretch you and make you the guitar player you've always wanted to be!

Take a look at the list below. Play around with it and see what other songs you can pick up. Sure, some of them may have little changes here and there, and slightly more complicated rhythm patterns. But, with the knowledge that you know have, you should be able to make them sound very similar if not spot on!

They will work with many different patterns, but some are better suited than others, so we'll let you know which one to try.

> **EXTENDED DEADLINE:** *You may practice the above songs for a day or two before getting to the below songs*

Bonus Songs

A quick interruption in our scheduled program! This part of the book is an update after the initial book was released. I decided to add a few more songs for you and have also provided backing tracks to play along.

You can find the audio version and the backing tracks for the below tracks in the bonus section of the book.

Here is a link to the video version — **http://bit.ly/songs-melodies**

Beginner Song 1

Beginner Song 2

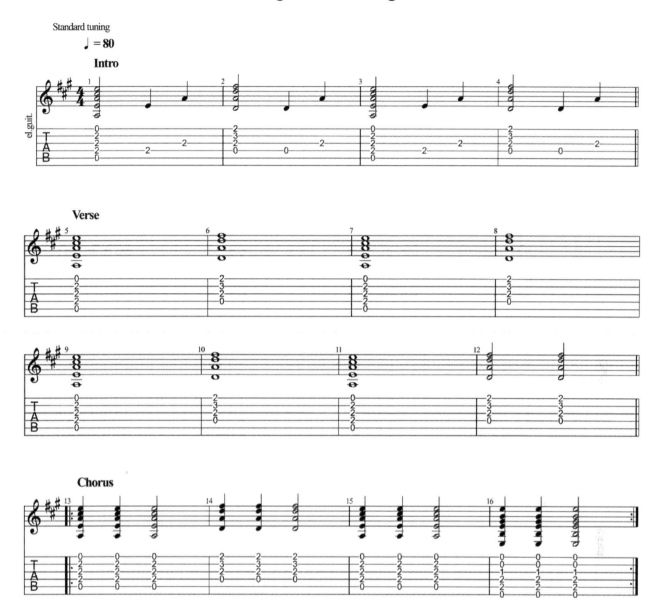

Beginner Song 3

Other Popular Songs You Can Play

"The Tide is High" by Blondie

An excellent simple song that is best played with mainly downstrokes.

"I Can't Explain" by The Who

A classic from The Who with a simple rhythm. We would suggest using either all downstrokes or the second half of Rhythm Pattern 4 over each chord for this one. The song is played using Palm Muting, which involves resting your palm very gently on the strings. Don't worry about this, for now, get the chords and the rhythm down first, then move on to that.

"Born This Way" by Lady Gaga

Easy chords, easy rhythm — easy does it!

Many people play this song using a Capo. This is a device which is attached to the neck across all six strings. Its function is to raise the pitch of all the strings. So that when you play any chord it will be heard at a higher pitch than if you play it without a capo.

It is mainly used by singers who want to easily change the key of a song. In simple terms, that means... singers use it to make songs easier for them to sing. It can be adjusted from fret to fret to allow them to do this.

"Hound Dog" by Elvis Presley

Easy chords, average rhythm, but it is quite fast!

"Three Little Birds" by Bob Marley

A very simple song with a simple rhythm. For a beginner, it is best played with all downstrokes and if you want to make it sound more authentic, strum only the first few thicker strings on the odd beats — 1 and 3. And fuller downstrokes across all the higher strings on every even beat — 2 and 4.

There are a few small embellishments in the song which are created by hammering certain fingers down. But, don't worry about them for the moment. Get the rest down first and then move on to the musical bling!

"Wild Thing" by The Troggs

Another all-time classic, and so easy to play, just use two downstrokes on every chord.

It has a slightly more complicated bridge section which involves playing chords and then open strings. We suggest that you concentrate on getting the 'famous' bit down first, before moving on to the lesser known part.

"Authority Song" by John Mellancamp

Yet again, the same three simple chords but with a faster rhythm.

"Common People" by Pulp

A superb starter song! You can play it with mainly downstrokes and it stays on each chord for ages and ages... This gives you time to get your chords to sound perfect and get ready for the next chord change.

"Sympathy for the Devil" by The Rolling Stones — Verse section

What a great song and the verse only uses A, D, and E. The exact rhythm, however, will take you a while to get right. But, don't worry about that, just play it the closest you can for now while you get your chords down. As your ear develops, you will hear and understand harder rhythms easier and play them effortlessly.

The Chorus of the song contains a chord that we haven't covered, a B7, so leave that for now.

"Desire" by U2

There are some very fast chord changes in this one, but it's still the same 3 chords D, A and E. Well, not quite, instead of a D chord, The Edge uses a Dsus2, which is a D chord without the second finger. This is actually easier to play than a D chord due to the fact that it only uses two fingers not three.

As mentioned, this song motors along, but it's fine to slow it right down for now until you master the chord changes. Then speed it up slowly until your rocking it out!

Well done!

Well oh well...you did it!

I'm *super* proud of you! In just seven short days you learned more about guitar then most people would ever dream of. Even if you took more than 7 days — you're now better than most people who have picked up a guitar! You really should be proud of yourself! It's a pretty big accomplishment, that's for sure.

But the real exciting part is that this is only the tip of the iceberg. Learning to play the guitar has so much more to it that you may find yourself with a drive and desire to learn all you can.

That's where Part 2 of this book comes in...

PART 2

Taking Your Playing to the Next Level...

What do I get to learn in the 2nd part?

Before we get into Part 2 of the book, I need to mention that the journey to becoming a great guitar player is a long one. And, to be honest, no one has ever mastered it in all its complexities. That's why even the greatest guitarists alive today still practice.

Therefore, the intention of this part of the book is not to give you "everything" you need to become a pro guitarist (if that's even possible).

This part of the book is focused on giving you a start and introduction into the multiple sub universes under guitar. You see, guitar and music are endless oceans of knowledge and discovery. Each topic of guitar — chords, scales, theory, composing etc. — have their own worlds to it. And it's your job to decide your universe, dive into it and discover your identity within it.

For example, I was lead guitarist who started with rock, then moved to blues and then into solo fingerstyle guitar. Each of those phases took years of my life!

So, it's my job to give you the basics of what's possible through the second part of the book. We'll learn more about chords, rhythm, and scales.

By the time you're done with it — your heart will lead you to the next step. You might want to dive into the world of blues or the world of rhythm guitar or be the best shredder the world has seen. Or you might simply want to learn a few country chords to jam around a campfire.

Any of those is absolutely fine — it's you who gets to decide. The style that aligns the most with the person you are is the one you'll end up choosing.

Once you have made that choice, you can look for our book dedicated to that topic and go all out. At the time of writing this book, we have specialized series of books on topics such as guitar scales, guitar chords, blues guitar, bass guitar etc. You can check around if they're for you and get your hands on one of those.

So, sit down... strap yourself in... and let's get into Part 2 of the book and start taking your guitar playing to the next level!

CHAPTER 1

Other Open Chords... (Yes, There's More!!)

Major Chords

You should be well on the way to mastering your first three major chords — A, D, and E — by now, so let's look at several other open Major chords. These are called C Major (or C) and G Major (or G).

(Audio Tracks are available for all the chord charts)

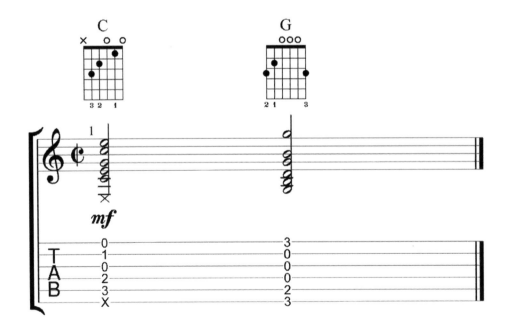

C Major (C)

G Major (G)

They are slightly harder to play than the first three chords because they involve more stretching, but in exactly the same way as happened when you learned A, D, and E, you'll be amazed at how quickly they start sounding good and become easier to play.

And remember, while you're learning them, follow the steps we outlined in Part 1 of the book. First off, just get your fingers used to the position, then when that's comfortable, strum one of the basic rhythm patterns over the chord and change to a chord you already know well, then change back to the new chord. Once you get the hang of that, play every note of the new chord individually to make sure it sounds good, when they all do, strum it to make sure that they all sound great together as well!

And there's some other great news as well, the more chords you learn, the easier and quicker it is to play new ones. So, as you're practicing the C and G, think about how much easier it is to learn the chords you don't even know the names of yet, because your fingers will just start finding their way around the guitar as if by magic!

Minor Chords

We did mention these very briefly in Part 1, but now it's time to learn them! As we said, they sound much sadder than Major chords and are great for adding a melancholy feel to chord progressions.

The three minor chords we will be learning are A minor (or Am), D minor (or Dm) and E minor (or Em).

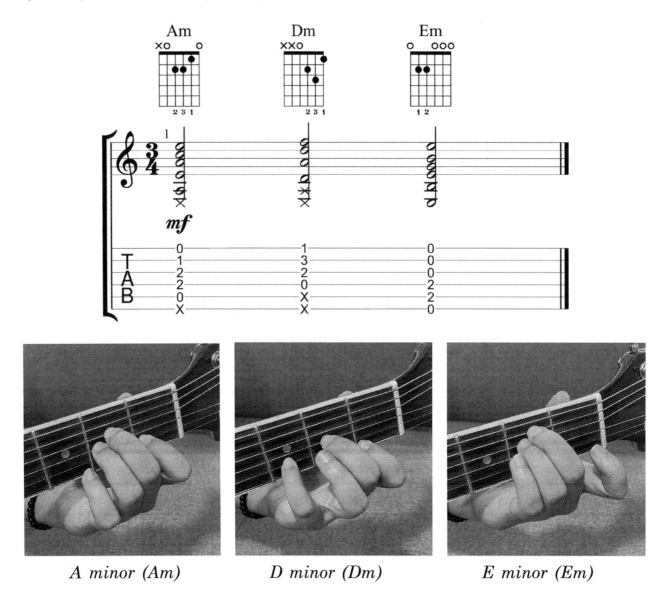

A minor (Am)   *D minor (Dm)*   *E minor (Em)*

You should find A minor very easy to play, it is exactly the same shape as an E major, but every finger is positioned one string lower on the fretboard — it's an E down a string!

E minor is even easier, it's an E Major chord without the first finger. You can play it with either your second and third fingers as if you were playing an E Major but not using your first finger. Or you can play it with your first and second fingers. There is no right or wrong way, it normally depends on the song you're playing as to which fingering you use.

The last minor chord is D minor, which is quite a bit harder to play than the other two minor chords and will take a lot more work to sound good. But it's well worth it, it's a wonderful chord and as the great Nigel Tuffnel said in the classic movie 'This is Spinal Tap', "it's part of a trilogy, a musical trilogy that I'm doing in D... minor, which I always find is really the saddest of all keys, really, I don't know why. It makes people weep instantly. And who doesn't want to learn a chord that makes people "weep instantly"?

And don't forget to listen to the accompanying audio files to make sure that everything is sounding exactly as it should.

Dominant Seventh Chords

These are chords that add character and emphasis to a chord progression or song. They are created by adding a minor seventh to a Major chord. Adding a what to a what??? You must be thinking? I just sneaked a little bit of music theory in there so I can reference it later... But, don't worry, you don't need to understand why these chords are what they are at the moment. It's not important at this stage, just learn how to play them well and make them sound great!

The chords we will be learning are A Dominant Seventh (A7), C Dominant Seventh (C7), D Dominant Seventh (D7), E Dominant Seventh (E7), and G Dominant Seventh (G7).

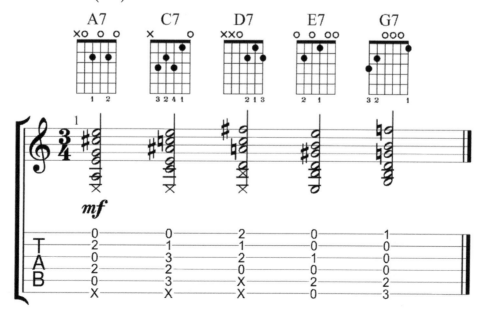

Some of these chords are easy to play and others are harder, for example, a C7 is the first chord you've played so far that uses all four fingers. So, let's go through them one by one...

A7

A Dominant 7th (A7)

This is easy, it's a normal A Major chord, but without the second or middle finger. It is normally played using the first and third fingers. However, like the Em chord, it can be played with the first and second fingers or second and third fingers, if that suits a particular song.

C7

C Dominant 7th (C7)

Even though this uses four fingers, it's actually quite easy after you learn how to play a C Major chord well. Simply play that C Major chord then add your little finger on the G string on the third fret.

D7

D Dominant 7th (D7)

Again, this is quite easy to play. If you think of a D shape as a triangle, as I do, then a D7 is the same triangle but going in the opposite direction. You, therefore, place your first finger on the B string on the first fret, your second finger on the G string on the second fret, and your third finger on the high E string on the second fret.

E7

E Dominant 7th (E7)

This is very easy. In the same way, as an Em was an E major chord without the first finger, an E7 chord is an E Major chord without the third finger. I did say that the more chords you know, the easier it gets!

And finally, for this chapter on all the open chords, we have a...

G7

G Dominant 7th (G7)

And, it's time to get all stretchy again. First finger on the first fret of the high E string, second finger on the second fret of the A string (told you it was a stretch!) and the third finger on the third fret of the low E string (ouch!).

So, there you have them, all the open chords you'll need to play a massive selection of songs. And when you consider how many great songs you could play using only A, D, and E, with all these extra chords, the world is your lobster, or is it oyster??? Anyway, something like that?

Bonus Songs

Again, an update to the book. You know how the drill goes by now!

Same as before – audio version and backing tracks in the bonus section; tabs below and a link to the video version of the song - http://bit.ly/songs-melodies

Beginner Song 4

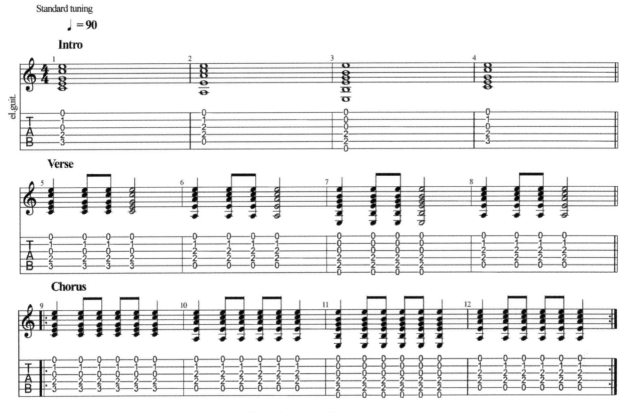

Beginner Song 5

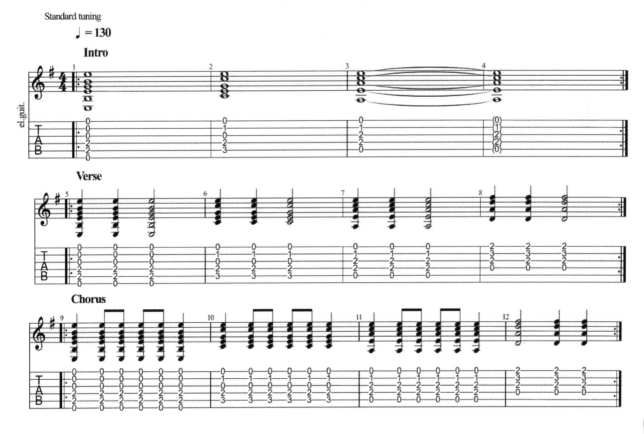

Beginner Song 6

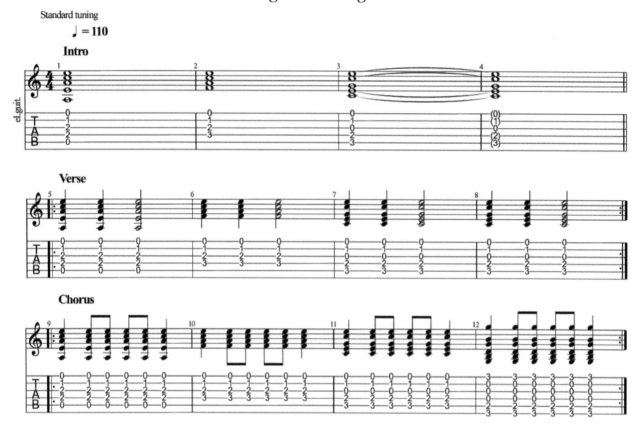

Other popular songs to play using all these new chords

Well, there are so many, that I'm not quite sure where to start. But here are ten to get you going...

Knocking on Heavens Door by Bob Dylan, Guns and Roses and just about everyone else as well can be played using only G, D, and Am, throwing in a C to replace the Am here and there.

What a Wonderful World by Sam Cook is basically G, Em, C, and D for the verse and chorus, with a few A7's and D7's thrown into the bridge for good measure!

Stuck in the Middle with You by Stealers Wheel can be played by using D, G7, A, C, and G.

The One I Love by R.E.M. is easily tackled using only Em, Dsus2 (a D major without the second finger, like we used in Desire by U2 in Part 1 of this book), Em7. Along with G, D, Am, and C.

Mull of Kintyre by Wings only uses A, D, E for most of the song, with a G added for the third and final choruses.

Brown Eyes Girl by Van Morrison is a breeze if you use a few G's, C's, and D's with an occasional Em and D7 thrown in!

Zombie by The Cranberries has a few slight alterations on the chords here and there, but on the whole, you can play it using Em, C, G, and D all the way through.

Honkey Tonk Woman by The Rolling Stones - just mix up a few G's, C's, A's, and D's and you'll be playing it like Keiff!

Ain't No Sunshine by Bill Withers is basically a lot of Am, with some occasional Em, G, and Am's thrown in and a Dm here and there to add some interest!

All of Me by John Legend - It's amazing what you can do with Em, C, G, and D, and since you just played them over and over on Zombie, this should be no trouble at all. Throw in an Am in the song's Bridge and Chorus and you too will be a Legend!

CHAPTER 2

Rhythm and Strumming

Rhythm is the word that musicians use to describe the passage of time in music. Rhythm is all around you. Every single thing in this universe follows a specific rhythm. As soon as you recognize this, you will begin to hear music all around you, all the time!

Your heart beats at different rhythms throughout the day, faster when excited and slower when resting. You have a circadian rhythm that governs when you sleep and when you wake, which is affected by the celestial rhythms of the sun and moon. You also have a rhythm to your walking, to your speech, and even to your eating, blinking, and breathing patterns.

There are many words used to describe rhythms. Words like tempo, time signature, and measure all describe a different aspect of rhythm and how rhythms are organized into music. In music, we notate rhythm on the staff using different styles and shapes of notes and rests. Remember that notes mark pitches (sounds we hear) and that rests are used to mark silence (no sounds).

It is important to understand that even silence has a rhythm. In fact, the absence of sound is a major clue to unlocking the rhythm of a particular piece of music.

How to Begin to Understand Rhythm in Music

The easiest way to begin to understand how rhythms work in music is to learn about the different types of notes and rests. The shape that a note or rest takes determines how long the rhythm will last. Musicians are like secret mathematicians. Each note or rest receives a specific number of counts and so musicians train themselves to constantly count the beats as the music moves.

If you have ever found yourself tapping your foot to a song, dancing to a beat, or been in a crowd at a concert where the band has the audience clap along then you are already intuitively familiar with counting rhythms in music. The next step is to bridge your intuition into reality.

The Different Types of Notes and Their Rhythms

There are four main types of notes you will learn here. Each note consists of some combination of a note head, a note stem, and potentially a dot on the right hand side or a beam or flag to connect it to other notes. We will move slowly through these so that you understand everything, don't worry!

The Whole Note

This is a whole note:

A whole note is an open note head with no stem, dot, flag, or beam. It basically looks like an oval on the staff. Some people call it a doughnut. Yum doughnuts …

But seriously, the whole note lasts for four counts. You will learn more about how measures are organized by time signatures in a moment. For now, just understand that a whole note lasts four counts.

The Dotted Half Note

The next note is called the dotted half note. It looks like this:

A dotted half note features an open note head, a stem, and a dot on the right hand side. All of these features combine to define the dotted half note. The dotted half note lasts for 3 counts. The dot on the right hand side is super significant, more on that later.

The Half Note

Next up is the glorious half note. A half note looks like this:

A half note features an open note head with a stem. There is no dot, flag, or beam connected to the half note. The half note lasts for two counts.

The Significance of the Dot

Did you figure out the significance of the dot marking? The only visual difference between the half note and the dotted half note is the dot marking on the right hand side. The half note lasts for two counts and the dotted half note lasts for three. So what function does that dot serve?

The dot on the right hand side of a note adds one half of the note value to the rhythm. So for example, a half note receives two counts. ½ of 2 equals 1. 2 plus 1 equals 3. So a half note with a dot (dotted half note) receives three counts. Make sense? I told you that musicians are secret mathematicians!

The Quarter Note

Next, we move to the quarter note. The quarter note looks like this:

The quarter note features a closed note head (the first example!) and a stem. There is no dot here or beam. A quarter note receives one count. Simple and elegant.

The Eighth Note

The final type of note we will learn now is the eighth note. The eighth notes look like this:

Eighth notes can appear two different ways. The first example on the left is of a single eighth note. A single eighth note features a closed note head, a stem, and a flag that hangs from the stem. This flag is what differentiates a single eighth note from a quarter note.

The example on the right is of two eighth notes. When two eighth notes are played together, a beam is used to connect them. You will also see groups of four eighth notes beamed together.

A single eighth note lasts for $^1/_2$ of a count. That means that it takes two eighth notes to equal 1 count.

Two eighth notes equal one quarter note. Two quarter notes equal one half note. Two half notes equal one whole note. See how all this lines up? It is quite neat.

The Different Types of Rests and Their Rhythms

For each type of note to mark a particular pitch, there is a corresponding rest to mark the same length of silence as the note. There are four main types of rests that you will learn here.

The Whole Rest

The whole rest is analogous to the whole note. It looks like this:

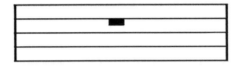

The whole rest is a closed rectangle that hangs down from the fourth line of the staff. Remember, the staff is the collection of five lines and four spaces that music is notated on. Like the whole note, the whole rest receives four counts.

The Half Rest

The half rest is analogous to the half note. It looks like this:

There are two half rests in the picture above. A half rest is a closed rectangle that sits on top of the third line of the staff. The half rest lasts for two counts.

There are not as many examples of a dotted half rest in music as there are examples of dotted half notes. More frequently, you will see the combination of a half rest and a quarter rest.

The Quarter Rest

The quarter rest is analogous to the quarter note and looks like this:

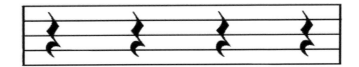

There are four quarter rests in the image above. A quarter rest looks like a 'Z' with a backwards 'c' attached to the bottom. What a strange shape!

Like the quarter note, the quarter rest receives one count.

The Eighth Rest

Finally, we come to the eighth rest. The eighth rest is analogous to the eighth note and looks like this:

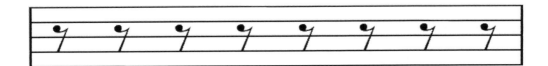

There are eight, eighth rests in this measure. Try saying that eight times fast!

The eighth rest looks like a fancy '7' and, like the eighth note, lasts for ½ of a count. However, unlike the eighth note, you will never see eighth rests beamed together. In fact, you will never see any type of rest beamed together like you will see notes beamed together.

Here is a handy diagram that connects all the different types of notes and rests together:

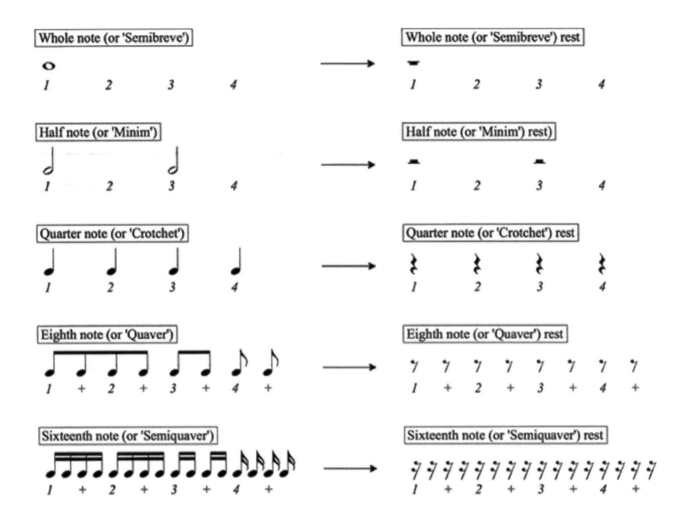

What Exactly is a Time Signature?

Musicians use a tool called a time signature to help organize rhythms. A time signature is a combination of two numbers that appear on the staff stacked on top of one another. Understanding time signatures is crucial to unlocking the ways that music is notated.

4/4 Time Signature

We will take a look at two examples of time signatures here. The first time signature is called 4/4, pronounced "four-four." 4/4 is one of the most common time signatures. For this reason, 4/4 is also known as common time.

The time signature for 4/4 looks like this on the staff:

The time signature tells us two important pieces of information. First, the top number tells us how many beats or counts are inside of every measure. Remember, a measure is the basic building block of notated music. If you are unclear, here are a few examples of measures:

The vertical lines above are called measure lines or bar lines. Those vertical lines are like little cells of music. The top number of the time signature tells us how many counts will fit inside of each cell.

This means that in a 4/4 time signature, there are four beats inside of every measure. This is a basic fundamental of music notation, sort of like 1+1=2 in math.

The bottom number of the time signature is slightly more esoteric than the top number. The bottom number of the time signature tells us which type of note will receive 1 count in the measure. In other words, the bottom number tells us which type of note will be our basic unit of counting.

When the bottom number is 4, this means the quarter note will receive one count. In time signatures with 4 on the bottom, the quarter note is the basic count. So for example, in a 4/4 time signature, each measure will have four beats and the quarter note will receive one count. Here is a visual of what this looks like:

3/4 Time Signature

The second time signature we will look at is called 3/4, pronounced "three-four." Can you take what you learned from the 4/4 time signature and apply it to 3/4? How many beats are inside of each measure in 3/4 time?

There are three beats inside of each measure in 3/4 time because the top number is three. Remember, the top number tells us how many beats are inside each measure.

Which type of note will receive one count in a 3/4 time signature? The bottom number is four, which tells us that the quarter note will also receive one count in 3/4 time. Check out this visual below to see this all laid out:

There are three beats inside each measure and the quarter note receives one beat in a 3/4 time signature.

Some Examples of Counting and Strumming

Now that you have a basic grip on the concepts of rhythms, notes, rests, and time signatures, let's try to apply some of this new knowledge to strumming patterns using some of the chords you learned in Part 1!

Strumming Downbeats in 4/4 Time

First, we will try some counting and strumming examples in 4/4 time using the chords A major, D major, and E major.

The first example we will look at uses only down strokes. Down strokes are most commonly placed on the downbeats of a measure. For example, in a measure of 4/4, the downbeats occur on beats 1, 2, 3, 4. Check out the example below to get started:

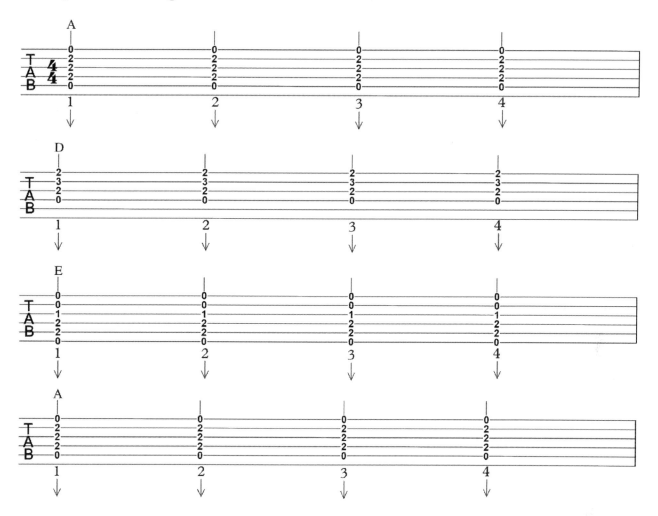

All of the down arrows below the chords indicate where you should strum a downstroke. Do you see how all of these downstrokes fall on the downbeats (beats 1, 2, 3, 4)? There is a strong feeling of gravity to these downbeats. Try to tune into this gravity with your downstroke strums.

Strumming Downbeats in 3/4 Time

Now let's try strumming and counting some downbeats in 3/4 time. This exercise is quite similar to the last one, so we will change up the chord progression a little bit. The same rules apply: when you see a down arrow, this means you do a downstroke. All the downstrokes will fall on the downbeats. Check out the diagram below to play it out!

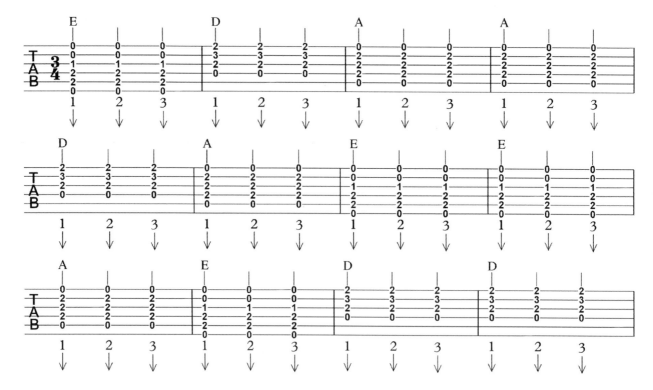

There are a few more chord changes in this example, but the same principle applies. Do you see how all the downstrokes fall on down beats? It is important to become very comfortable with this feeling. These two exercises are also a great way to become comfortable counting in 4/4 and 3/4 time signatures, which is a crucial skill to develop as a musician.

Strumming and Counting With Eighth Notes

Now that you have some understanding of strumming with downstrokes to count and feel the downbeats in 4/4 and 3/4 time signatures, let's check out how we can use upstrokes to count and feel eighth notes.

Remember that eighth notes last for ½ of one beat. This means that it takes two eighth notes to make one entire beat. It also means it takes two eighth notes to make a quarter note. So we will need some additional symbols to account for these added notes.

Remember that eighth notes can be beamed in groups of two and four, so don't let that throw you off. This is how you count eighth notes in a measure of 4/4 time:

We use the "+" symbol to account for these extra notes and we pronounce it as "and." To count this measure, say "1 — and — 2 — and — 3 — and — 4 — and."

The notes with the + symbol are on the upbeats. The upbeats happen between the downbeats. You can also visualize this like a wave. Waves have crests and waves of troughs. Music has downbeats and music has upbeats. There are moments when the momentum is moving downward and then there are moments when the momentum moves upward. This tension between down and upbeats is what pushes music along and is a huge part of what makes music interesting to listen to.

To strum eighth notes, we will use a combination of downstrokes and upstrokes. The downstrokes will fall on the downbeats, like they did when we practiced the quarter notes. The upstrokes will land on the upbeats, or the "ands" of each beat. "Ands" is a word you will hear musicians use to refer to the offbeats or upbeats.

Check out this example of strumming eighth notes in 4/4 time:

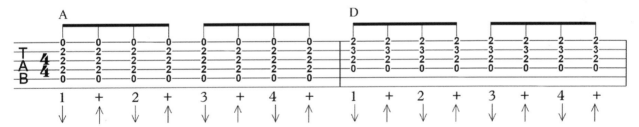

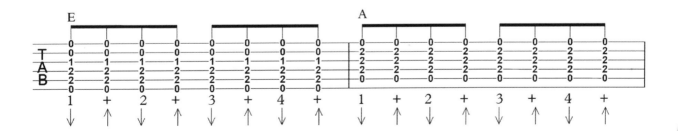

Do you see how all the upstrokes fit with the upbeats? Practicing connecting the physical motion of an upstroke with the rhythmic feeling of an upbeat. Building and strengthening this connection will help you develop a strong feel of musical time.

Here is an example of strumming eighth notes in 3/4 time:

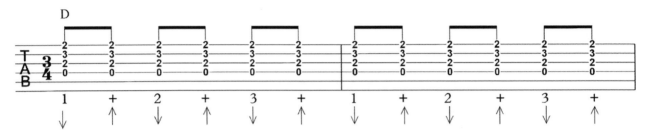

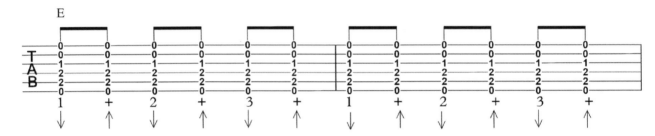

Once again, pay special attention to the connection between the physical motion of an upstroke with the rhythmic feeling of an upbeat. This feeling is what propels music forward. The more you can connect yourself physically to rhythms, the stronger your feeling for rhythm will become.

Some Basic Patterns to Practice

Now that you understand how to strum and count quarter notes and eighth notes in 4/4 and 3/4 times signatures and are building a strong connection between the physical motion of your strums and the down and upbeats, let's take a look at some common strumming patterns. We will keep using these three chords: A major, D major, and E major.

Check out this practice strumming pattern in 4/4 time:

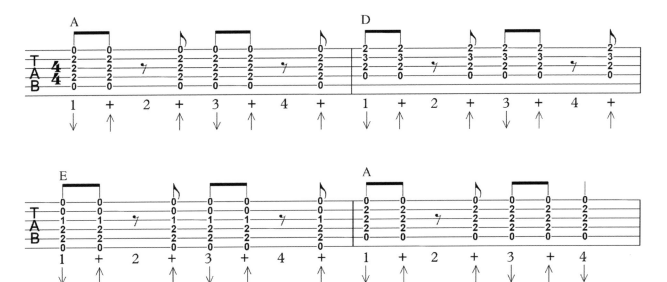

Pay attention in the above example to how the upstroke on the "and" of beats 2 and 4 falls into the downstroke on the downbeats of 1 and 3. This is a great strumming pattern to build that feeling.

Check out this practice strumming pattern in 3/4 time:

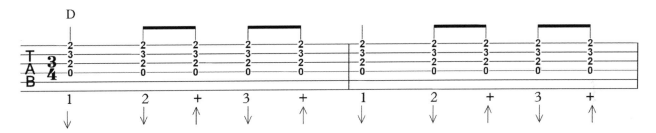

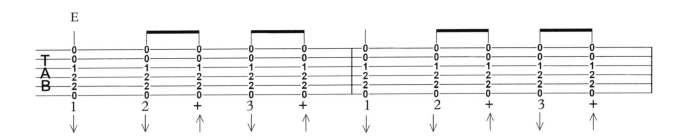

CHAPTER 3

F chord and B chord

There are many layers of chords to explore on the guitar. You can spend countless hours learning different inversions and patterns and how to create smooth sounding progressions using voice-leading.

However, you need to have a few more basic chord shapes under your fingers before it really makes sense to dive into that deeper work. Fortunately, there are a couple of systems unique to the guitar that make learning chords easier than learning chords on a piano, for example.

On guitar, we have the ability to play one chord shape and move that same chord shape up or down the fretboard to change the root note of the chord. On the piano, for example, every chord has a different shape, and to play all 12 major chords in root position requires you to memorize 12 different chord shapes!

However, this simplicity in chord shapes comes with a trade off. Many guitar chords use a more difficult hand position that requires you to hold down more than one string with one finger. We call this technique "barring" and chords that use this technique "barre" chords or "bar" chords. Barre chords may feel difficult when you first try them, but with steady practice you will find that they are quite easy and extremely useful in a number of situations.

Some Basic Chord Shapes

Mini-Barre F Major Chord

Now let's dive into some basic chord shapes. The first shape we will learn is an F major triad in first position. Check out the chord diagram below:

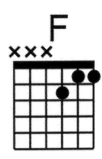

The root of this chord is on F on the first fret of the high E string. To make this chord, place your second finger (your middle finger) on the second fret of the G string and then play the first fret on both the B string and high E string with your first finger (your index finger). Nice work! This is a mini-barre chord because you have barred the first fret on two strings with your first finger.

Mini-Barre B Major Chord

Now let's check out another mini-barre major chord shape. Check out the diagram below for this B major triad on the D, G, and B strings:

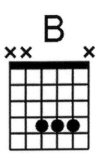

The root of this chord is on B on the 4th fret of the G string. There are two ways to make this chord. You can make this chord by covering the entire 4th fret with your first or third finger. That is probably the easiest method.

You can also make this chord by placing your first finger on the 4th fret of the D string, second finger on the 4th fret of the G string, and third finger on the 4th fret of the B string. This method requires a little more coordination.

Full-Barre F Major Chord

The mini-barre F major chord can be expanded to a full-barre chord by making few additional steps. Instead of a barre on the top two strings, you will reposition your hand to barre the entire first fret with your third finger. This can be a little bit difficult for beginners, but if you stick with it, you will be well rewarded!

Check out this diagram of an F major full-barre chord:

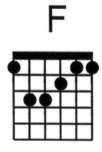

The root of this chord is found on F on the first fret of the low E string. To play this chord shape, cover the entire first fret with your first finger, then place your third finger on the 3rd fret of the A string, your fourth finger on the 3rd fret of the D string, and your second finger on the 2nd fret of the G string. When you strum this chord shape, you want to strum all 6 strings.

Full-Barre B Major Chord

The mini-barre B major chord can also be expanded to a full-barre chord with the root on the 2nd fret of the A string. Check out the diagram below to learn the shape:

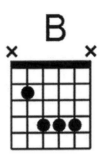

The easiest way to play this chord shape is to barre the entire 4th fret with your third finger and then place your first finger on the 2nd fret of the A string. When you strum this chord shape, strum the middle 4 strings.

Let's improve the chord with an exercise

In order to practice this, we will start playing bars without the rest of the chord and will add one string at a time. Begin by playing two strings at the same time on the same fret using your index finger. Try each string individually. If they ring out correctly, add the 3rd string. If it works, continue with four strings. Keep going until you have all six strings producing a great sound.

The bad news is that you are probably using tremendous strength to keep everything ringing clearly. The good news is that you don't really need to use that much strength. Try to use as little finger pressure as possible while still having the notes sound as they should.

Have another look at the shapes — you are never really pressing on more than 4 strings at a time, and in fact most of the times we just have to play 2 or 3 of them at the same time with one finger. The others are covered by your fingers higher up on the neck. So, we are going to try to focus the strength of our finger on those strings where it's needed. This is the key to making them all work together!

Now, of course, you will need to apply the same principles as before. Practice one at a time, then try to connect them using the strumming patterns.

Move them around...

Take the same fingering that you used for the F Major chord and move your fingers up two frets (where your index finger is covering entire 3rd fret). You now have a G Major chord! Slide it up two more frets and you have an A Major chord, etc.

Same thing you can do with your B Major chord. Move a fret above and you have a C Major chord, Slide it up two more frets and you have D Major chord.

Here are some more...

Songs for practicing your F chord include House of the Rising Sun by The Animals, just add some Am's, C's, D's and the odd E and you'll be swinging!

Or try Let it Be by The Beatles, again add C, G, and Am.

Another great song to get your F chord down is The Passenger by Iggy Pop, just play an Am, F, C, followed by a G the first time around and the same sequence, but followed by an E the second time around - all the way through!

Or if you want something more modern, how about Let Her Go by Passenger (see what I did there? Clever eh!), anyway, mix up quite a bit of G, F, G, and Am. And throw in a little C in the chorus and you'll traveling like a Wilbury!

Sticking with the modern theme, how about Rolling in the Deep by Adele. For the verse, Am, Em, and G with some repeats are all you need. Then add in an F in the pre-chorus and the chorus and you'll be playing it well. The only question is... can you sing it as well as her?

That's quite enough F chord songs for you, so let's finish up this chapter with some B's.

Let's start off with Alanis Morrisette's Hand in my Pocket. To play this all you'll need is good old A, D and E, and of course a few B chords!

Or, if you like the chords but are not a big fan of Alanis, you can use the exact same ones to play the excellent No Rain by Blind Melon.

CHAPTER 4

What is a Scale?

Have you ever heard of the musical scale? In music, a scale is a collection of notes organized in ascending order by pitch. That means that a scale begins with a note, for example C, and then each note after C is higher in pitch, until the scale arrives at C again, one octave higher. Remember, one octave is the distance between a note and the next highest or lowest note with the same letter name.

There are literally hundreds of different types of scales. You can spend a lifetime learning and understanding scales. Many people have done this and we are fortunate now to be studying music at a point in time where we have access to centuries of discoveries. I view the different types of scales like different colors or types of paint; each color has its purpose and place and causes a particular effect.

The Musical Alphabet

However, before we can dive too much deeper into the world of scales, we need to lay some foundational information to guide our way. One important piece of information is called the musical alphabet. Yes, we have our own alphabet in music.

The musical alphabet is: **A, B, C, D, E, F, G**.

The musical alphabet begins with A and moves to G. After G, the alphabet begins again from A. This pattern continues as high and as low as the guitar goes. For example, the lowest note you can play on the guitar in standard tuning is E (the open low E string) and the highest note you can play is generally D (the 22nd fret of the high E string). All the other notes fit inside these boundaries on the guitar.

Check out these notes on the fret board:

```
T
A  7
B  4 ─0─────────2─────────3─────────0─────────2─────────3─────────0──────
       A         B         C         D         E         F         G
```

You will need to be able to readily recall the musical alphabet inside your head at any given moment, forwards and backwards. Yes, to learn the deeper mysteries of music you will need to be able to think the alphabet backwards as well!

But Aren't There More Notes Than That?

You might be wondering at this point, aren't there more than 7 notes? Yes, you correct there are more than 7 notes in music. There are in fact 12 notes in the tuning system we use. This tuning system is called equal temperament. We are not going to dive into equal temperament here, as it would take a while to explain it in detail.

Suffice it to say that equal temperament divides the octave in 12 equal pieces, so each octave has 12 notes inside of it. There are many different tuning systems all over the world. If you are curious, it is a fascinating subject to explore!

Sharps and Flats

So how is it that we account for these additional notes? If there are seven notes in the musical alphabet and 12 notes inside of an octave, how is this even possible?

We use two symbols to account for these additional notes. We call these symbols sharp and flat. The sharp symbol looks like this: ♯. The sharp symbol raises a note by one half step, the same distance as one fret on the guitar. For example if you see the note C:

You know that this note is on the first fret of the B string. Then if you see the sharp symbol before the note:

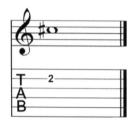

It means that the note is raised by one fret and is now found on the 2nd fret of the B string. Simple, right?

The opposite is true for the flat symbol. The flat symbol looks like this: ♭. The flat symbol means the note is lowered by one half step, or one fret. For example, if you see this note D:

You know that note is on the third fret of the B string. If we put the flat symbol before the note like this:

You can see that this note is one fret below D, on the second fret of the B string. Simple right?

Check out these sharp and flat notes on the fretboard:

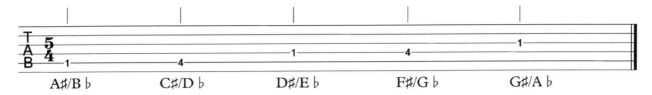

So How Does This All Add Up?

Now that you understand the musical alphabet and the ideas of sharps and flats, let's smash it all together. These are the twelve notes we have in equal temperament:

A, A#/Bb, B, C, C#/Db, D, D#/Eb, E, F, F#/Gb, G, G#/Ab

This scale with all twelve notes in it is called the "chromatic scale". Check out the chromatic scale on the fretboard below:

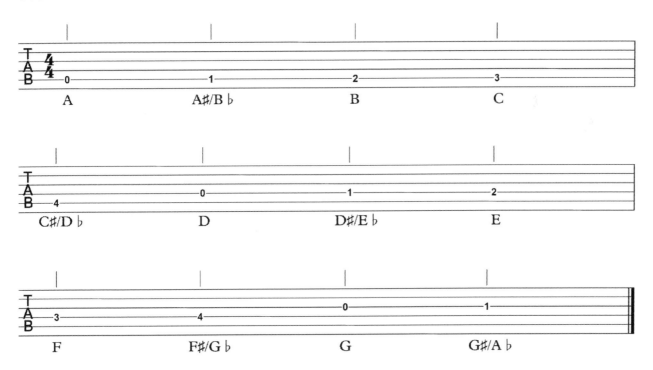

Imagine the chromatic scale as all the crayons in the box. You probably will not use all the crayons at any one time, but it is helpful to understand the full breadth of possibilities presented together. We will learn some exercises with the chromatic scale in Level 5.

A Quick Note on Measurements

In music we have a few different terms for measuring the distance between notes. You have already learned the word octave, meaning the distance between a note and the next highest or lowest note of the same letter name.

Another term you need to learn now is half step. One half step is the distance from one note to the next note higher or lower. For example, C to C♯ is one half step. The distance from F to F♯ is one half step. B to B♭ is one half step. A to A♭ is also one step.

One half step is equal to one fret on the guitar. From the first fret on the D string to the second fret on the D string is one half step. From the 7th fret on the G string to the 6th fret on the G string is one half step. The chromatic scale is built in half steps.

You will also need to know the term whole step. One whole step is equal to two half steps. For example, the distance from C to D is one whole step. From G to A is one whole step. From F♯ to G♯ is also one whole step. One whole step is equal to two frets on the guitar. From the fourth fret on the high E string to the sixth fret on the high E string is one whole step. From the tenth fret on the B string to the 12th fret on the B string in one whole step.

From 12 Back to 7

The next scale we will explore is called the major scale. The major scale is a 7 note scale that is extremely common. You have probably heard it, maybe you just don't know what it is called.

There is a formula for the major scale. Remember, musicians are secret mathematicians. There are patterns and formulas everywhere in music hiding behind the scenes.

The formula for the every major scale is:

whole step, whole step, half step,

whole step, whole step, wholes step, half step

Can you use the notes of the chromatic scale starting from C to figure out the first major scale?

If we start with C and move up one whole step, we reach D. One whole step above D is E. One half step above E is F. One whole step above F is G. One whole step above G is A. One whole step above A is B. And finally, one half step above B returns us to C, one octave higher than we began. Nice work!

Check out this pattern on the fretboard:

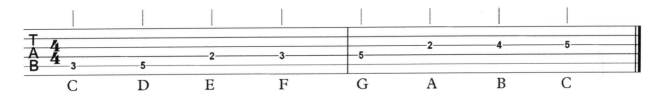

Practice this pattern up and down until you feel extremely comfortable with it. Do you notice anything special about this pattern? There are no sharp or flat notes in the C major scale. For this reason, the C major scale is often used as a good starting point for music theory work.

Once you feel comfortable with this pattern, extend the C major scale to two octaves starting from the eighth fret on the low E string. Check out this new pattern on the fretboard:

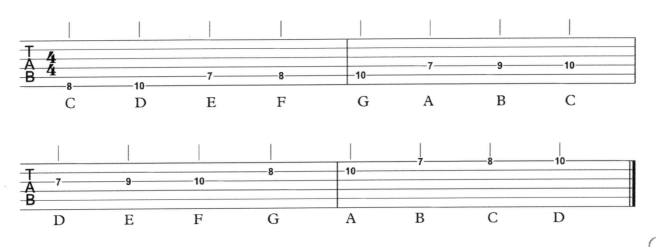

To play this pattern, begin with your second finger on C and follow the general rule of one finger for every fret. This means that any notes on the seventh fret will be played with your index finger, notes on the eighth fret with your middle finger, notes on the ninth fret with your ring finger, and notes on the tenth fret with your pinky.

Again, practice this pattern up and down until you feel very comfortable with it. Once you have memorized the pattern, try moving it to the keys of F, G, and A major.

Check out these examples below:

F major scale:

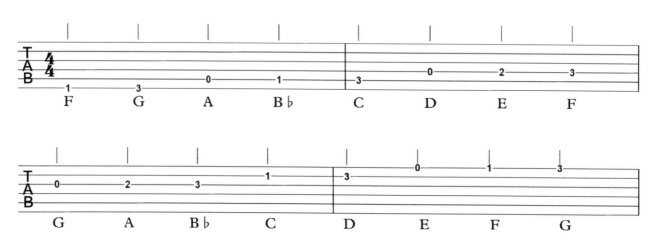

G major scale:

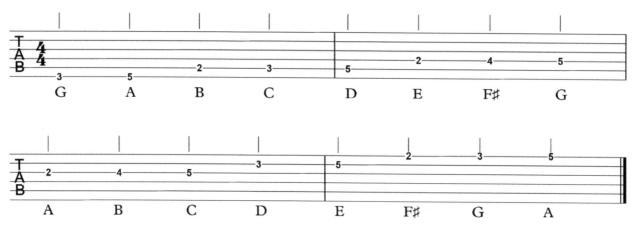

A major scale:

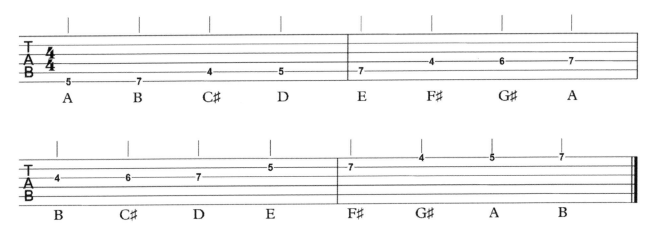

These are just four examples of the major scale. You can practice this pattern starting from any fret on the low E string!

Keys Unlock it All

The final piece we will uncover here in Level 3 is the concept of key and how scales and keys relate to one another.

In essence, a key is a way of organizing a group of notes into a hierarchy emerging from a fundamental note called the root. The root note of a key serves as a foundation and has a certain gravity to it. All notes in the key natural resolve to the root note.

You have already experienced this phenomenon with the major scales you practiced above and with the songs and chord progressions you practiced in Parts 1 and 2. You also hear this phenomenon in music all the time.

The Key Signature

The key signature is a shorthand notation system that musicians use. Understanding how a key signature works gives you a lot of valuable information about the music you are looking at. The key signature tells you which notes are automatically sharp or flat in the song. This means you know which chords and scales will sound good with the song and which chords and scales will sound bad.

The key signature is located on the right side of the staff, between the clef and the time signature. Here are two examples of key signature:

How Keys and Scales Work Together

Now let's combine our knowledge of scales with our knowledge of keys to get a glimpse of how these two concepts work together.

Let's start with the C major scale. Check out the notes of the C major scale. The notes of the C major scale are C — D — E — F — G — A — B — C. Are there any sharps or flats in the C major scale? No, there are no sharps or flats in the C major scale. This means that there are no sharps or flats in the key of C major. This means the key signature for C major looks like this:

Now let's check out the G major scale. Remember the notes of the G major scale are G — A — B — C — D — E — F♯ — G. There is one sharp in the

G major scale, F#. This means that the key of G major has one sharp, F#, which also means the key signature for G major is F#. Check this out below:

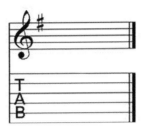

Does it make sense how we are connecting these dots? Let's try another one.

Now let's look at the key of F major. The notes of the F major scale are F — G — A — Bb — C — D — E — F. The F major scale has one flat, Bb. This means the key of F major has one flat, Bb, which also means the key signature for F major is a Bb. Check this out below:

One more example. Remember the A major scale from above? The notes of the A major scale are A — B — C# — D — E — F# — G# — A. This means that there are three sharps in the A major scale, C#, F#, and G#. This means that the key of A major has these three sharps, which also means the key signature for A major has these three sharps. The key signature for A major looks like this:

You can use this same process with all twelve major scales to find all twelve major key signatures!

CHAPTER 5

What are Intervals?

In Level 3 you were introduced to two terms that musicians use to measure distances between notes, half-step and whole-step. A half step is the distance from one note to the next higher or lower note. For example, from C to C♯ is one half step. A half step is the same thing as one fret up or down on the guitar neck. A whole step is equal to two half steps. For example, C to B♭ is one whole step. A whole step is equal to two frets up or down on the guitar.

So how do we account for distances greater than one or two notes? Musicians have another set of terms for these distances. We call them intervals.

You can think of an interval as the distance between any two notes. Intervals are counted in half steps and whole steps, but are described using a different set of terms. Intervals are described with a combination of two words such as perfect, major, minor, or diminished and second, third, fourth, fifth, etc. Let's dive into some intervals and learn a few tricks to hearing them!

A Quick Note on Playing Intervals

Some intervals are easier to play on the guitar than others. All intervals can be played two ways. If you see the term "melodic" intervals, this means that the intervals are played as in a melody. That is, one note after another. If you see the term "harmonic" intervals, this means that the intervals are played together as in a chord or harmony.

Intervals of a Second

There are two main types of intervals of a second: a minor second and a major second. Intervals are called "seconds" when the notes follow one another consecutively.

For example, any interval between E and F will be a second, any interval between G and A will be a second and any interval between C and D will be a second because all of those notes follow on another consecutively.

The terms perfect, major, minor, or diminished then refer to how many half steps are in an interval. For example, a minor second is equal to one half step. Minor seconds are easy to play melodically on the guitar. Here is an example reminiscent of the famous film score "Jaws":

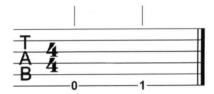

A major second is equal to two half steps, or one whole step. Here is an example of a major second on the guitar, from the melody "Happy Birthday":

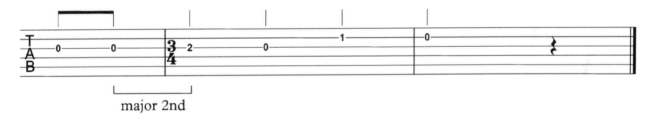

Intervals of a Third

Intervals of a third are three notes apart. Any interval between C and E, D and F, G and B, or F and A will be called a third. There are two main intervals of a third: a minor third and a major third.

A minor third is three half steps or three frets on the guitar. Check out this example of a minor third from the song "Smoke On The Water":

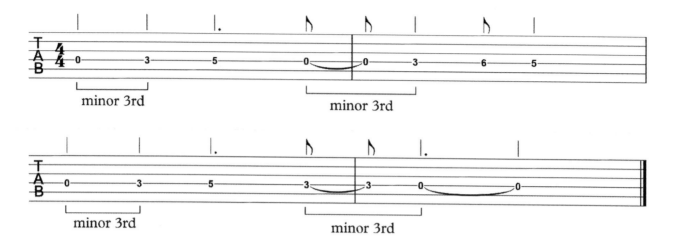

A major third is four half steps, the same thing as four frets on the guitar. Check out this example of a major third from the famous song "When The Saints Come Marching In":

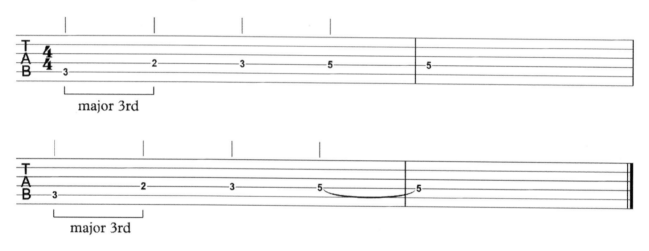

The Perfect Fourth

There are two perfect intervals, the perfect fourth and the perfect fifth. These intervals are called perfect because they have historically been heard as the most perfectly consonant intervals.

The perfect fourth is equal to 5 half steps. You can play a perfect fourth by stretching 5 frets on the fretboard or by playing the same fret on adjacent strings. In standard tuning, the strings of the guitar are all a perfect fourth apart, with the exception of the G and B strings, which are a major third apart. For example, from the 5th fret on the D string to the 5th fret on the G string is a perfect fourth.

Here is an example of a perfect fourth on the guitar from the melody "Amazing Grace":

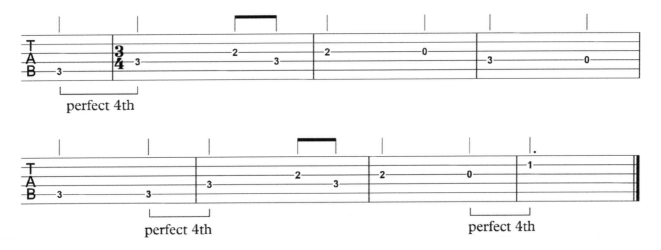

Intervals of a Fifth

There are two main types of intervals of a fifth, the diminished fifth and the perfect fifth. Any interval from C to G, D to A, or E to B etc. will be called a fifth because the notes are five letters apart.

The diminished fifth is 6 half steps or 6 frets horizontally on one string of the guitar. You can also make a diminished fifth by a diagonal ascending move from one string to the next. For example, from the 5th fret of the A string to the 6th fret of the D string is a diminished fifth and from the 4th fret of the low E string to the 5th fret of the A string is a diminished fifth.

Check out this example of a diminished fifth from the theme from "The Simpsons":

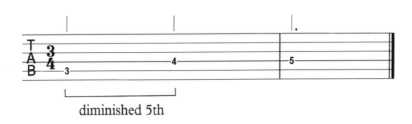

125

The second interval is called the perfect fifth. The perfect fifth is equal to seven half steps or 7 frets horizontally on the guitar. The perfect fifth is also the same thing as a two note power chord on the guitar. For example, if you play a G power chord on the 3rd fret of the low string to the 5th fret on the A string, that is a perfect fifth.

Check out this example of a perfect fifth on the guitar reminiscent of the theme from "Superman":

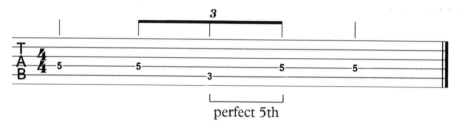

Intervals of a Sixth

Intervals of a sixth are six notes apart. From B to G, E to C, and A to F will all be some variety of a sixth. There are two types of sixth interval, the minor sixth and the major sixth.

The minor sixth is 8 half steps, or 8 frets on the guitar. You can also play a minor sixth by stretching one fret beyond a perfect fifth power chord. For example, from the 3rd fret of the low E string to the 6th fret of the A string is a minor sixth. It is a cool and dark sounding interval.

Check out this example of a minor sixth from the theme "1492" by Vangelis:

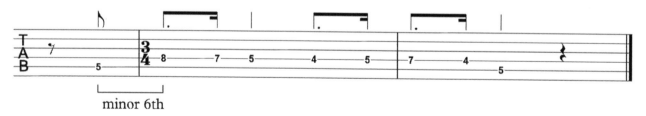

The major sixth is equal to 9 half steps, or 9 frets on the guitar. You can also play a major sixth from the 3rd fret of the low E string to the 2nd fret of the D string. Many guitarists also play major sixths between the G and high E strings. For example, from the 5th fret on the G string to the 5th fret on the high E string is a major sixth. You can slide this shape up and down for some cool effects.

Check out this example of a major sixth from "My Way" by Frank Sinatra:

Intervals of a Seventh

Intervals of a seventh are seven notes apart. For example, anything from C to B, D to C, or G to F will be called a seventh. There are two types of sevenths, the minor seventh and the major seventh.

The minor seventh is equal to 10 half steps, or 10 frets on the guitar. From the open low E string to the 10th fret is a minor seventh. You can also play minor sevenths on the same fret with a string skip in the middle. For example, from the 5th fret of the A string to the 5th fret of the D string is a minor seventh.

Here is an example of a minor seventh on the guitar from the theme from the original "Star Trek" series:

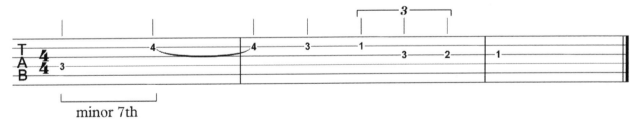

A major seventh is equal to 11 half steps, or eleven frets on the guitar. From the open low E string to the 11th fret is a major seventh. You can also find a major seventh from the 5th fret of the A string to the 6th fret of the D string or from the 7th fret of the G string to the 9th fret of the high E string.

Check out this example of a major seventh on the guitar from the classic chorus melody of "Take On Me" by a-ha:

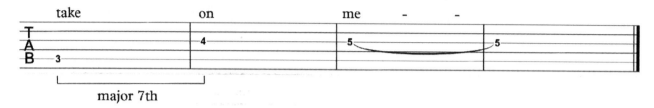

The Octave

Remember from Level 3, that one octave is the distance from one note to the next highest or lowest note of the same letter name. One octave is equal to 12 half steps, the same as 12 frets on the guitar. From any open string to the 12th fret on that string is one octave. You can also find an octave from the 5th fret of the low E string to the 7th fret of the D string or the 7th fret of the G string to the 10th fret on the high E string.

Check out this example of octaves on guitar from the tune "Let It Snow":

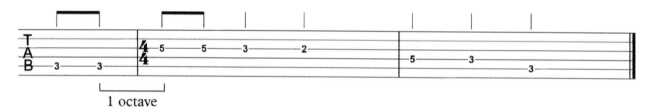

CHAPTER 6

Some Useful Exercises

Practicing the guitar (or any instrument for that matter) is very similar to practicing to be a great athlete. It is helpful to build routines and isolate certain sections of your playing to dial in any weaknesses you perceive. Additionally, it can be extremely useful to warm-up before practicing in the same sense that an athlete might stretch out or go for a light jog before beginning more difficult work. This helps energize the body and focus the mind so you can be more successful in your upcoming practice.

With all that in mind, here are a few warm-up exercises you can use to get your fingers connected and moving before you jam, practice, or play a gig! All these exercises are loosely based on the chromatic scale we learned in Level 3. Check them out!

Exercise 1:

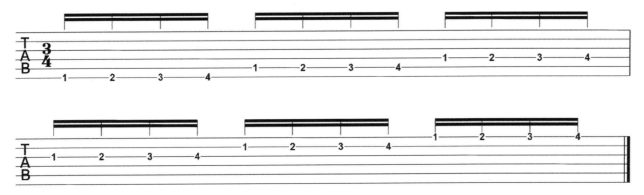

Begin this warm up on the first fret of the low E string with your first finger. Then, play one finger for every fret until you reach the fourth fret with your fourth finger. Continue this pattern up on the A string, D string, G string, B string, and high E string. You can then play the pattern in reverse if you wish. You can play this pattern up and down a few times in first position, or you can move it up and down the fretboard. This is a great warm up for getting your fingers and pick in tune with each other.

Alternate Picking

Ok — so we've covered how to hold the pick and where to place our right hand. Now it's time to start talking about something called "alternate picking".

So far, if you've used your pick in some way, you have most likely played in either exclusively downward or exclusively upwards motion with your pick, depending on what's more comfortable to you.

But remember how we were earlier only using downstrokes for strumming a chord but then we used a smart technique and started utilizing our arm movement even while coming up? Alternate picking is relatively the same. One down, one up. Or vice versa (up, then down) — we don't always have the luxury of starting the picking motion in our most comfortable direction, so it's a good idea to practice both.

Here is, once again, an exercise and the riffs we used to learn the "one finger per fret" principle. It's the same as it was except that we are going to also use for picking. As before, our left hand should follow every guideline we've covered, but this time we're going to concentrate on the right hand. You should start down, then move the pick back through the string going up. And then, go in reverse fashion. Up, then move the pick back down through the string.

Practice alternate picking with the following exercises:

Exercise 2:

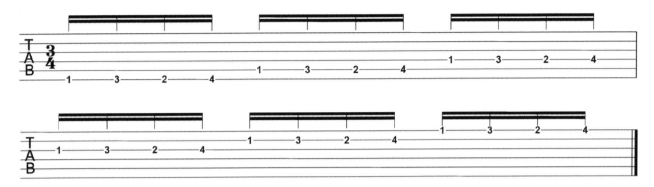

This is a great warm up for practicing coordination in your fret hand. Begin on the first fret of the low E string with your first finger, followed by the third fret with your third finger, second fret with your second finger, and fourth fret with your fourth finger.

Continue this pattern up the strings until you reach the high E string. Like Exercise 1, you can then practice this warm up in reverse or up and down the neck as you like.

Remember to practice these warm-ups slowly. They are warm ups, not sprints!

Exercise 3:

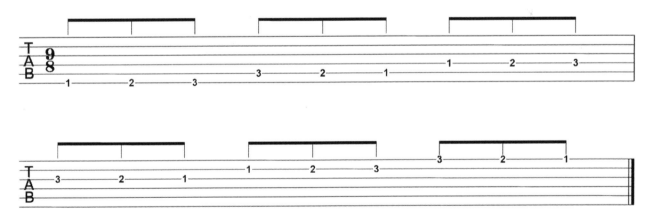

This warm up is a variation on Exercise 1 using only fingers 1, 2 and 3. Begin with your first finger on the first fret of the low E string, then play the second fret with your second finger, and third fret with your third finger. Next, shift up to the A string and begin with your third finger on the third fret, followed by your second finger on the second fret and finally your first finger on the first fret. Continue winding your way up the strings in this manner until you reach the high E string.

Exercise 4:

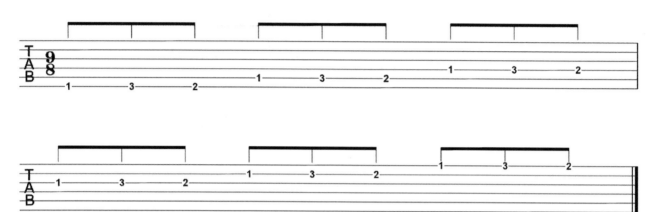

Exercise 4 is a little more complex and is a perfect coordination exercise to follow after these first 3 warm ups. The pattern is first fret/first finger, third fret/third finger, second fret/second finger, then shift up to the next string and repeat. Try to figure out the reverse pattern when you feel comfortable with this version.

Exercise 5:

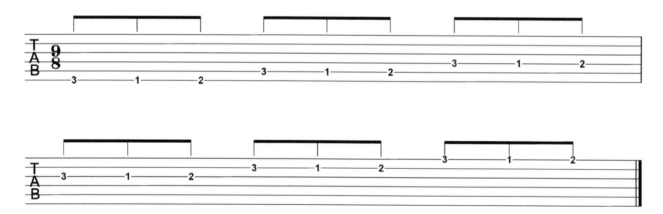

Exercise 5 is a variation on Example 4. Instead of beginning with your first finger on the first fret, begin with your third finger on the third fret, followed by first finger/first fret, then second finger/second fret. Continue this pattern up to the high E string.

Exercise 6:

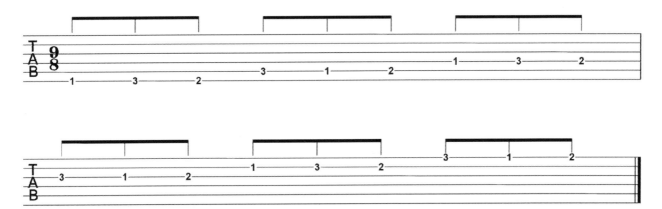

Exercise 6 is a combination of Exercises 4 and 5. Begin with your first finger on the first fret of the low E string, followed by third finger/third fret, then second finger/second fret. Shift up to the A string and begin with third finger/third fret, followed by first finger/first fret, then second finger/second fret. Continue this winding pattern up to the high E string.

Exercise 7:

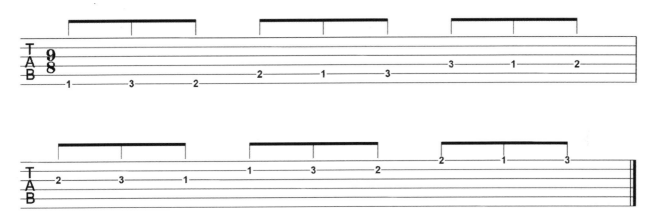

Exercise 7 is an example of what is possible when you combine all the different warm up exercises here with a little bit of imagination. The guitar is an endless maze of possibilities and all it takes is a little imagination to unlock new possibilities!

What Next?

Now that you've learned a few chords and scales, its time to spend some time practicing what you've learned.

Here's your next reading suggestion:

Guitar Exercises for Beginners

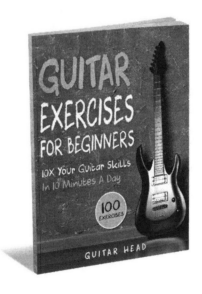

Guitar Exercises for Beginners will help you craft a practice routine that'll 10x your guitar skills in 10 minutes a day.

You can find it on our website.

Farewell!

Pssssttt....

What are you doing here? Are you lost?

Do people even look at the last pages of a book?

Jokes aside, I hope you enjoyed this book. I certainly loved the process of writing it.

If you enjoyed this book, could you take 2 minutes to leave a review about it?

Reviews are the lifeblood for small publishers and help us get our books into the hands of more guitarists like you.

We read every review personally and appreciate each one of it.

To leave a review, simply go to the platform you purchased the book from and type in your review.

With that said, here's Guitar Head signing off!

Until next time then? I'll see you in another book.

THE END

Printed in Poland
by Amazon Fulfillment
Poland Sp. z o.o., Wrocław